DISCARD

Education

Reference Sources
in the Social Sciences Series

Robert H. Burger, Series Editor

Psychology: A Guide to Reference and Information Sources.
By Pam M. Baxter.

American Military History: A Guide to Reference and Information Sources. By Daniel K. Blewett.

Sociology: A Guide to Reference and Information Sources.
Second Edition. By Stephen H. Aby.

Education: A Guide to Reference and Information Sources.
Second Edition. By Nancy Patricia O'Brien.

Education

A Guide to
Reference and Information Sources

Second Edition

Nancy Patricia O'Brien

University of Illinois at Urbana-Champaign

2000
LIBRARIES UNLIMITED, INC.
Englewood, Colorado

LIBRARIES UNLIMITED, INC.
P.O. Box 6633
Englewood, CO 80155-6633
1-800-237-6124
www.lu.com

Library of Congress Cataloging-in-Publication Data

O'Brien, Nancy P.
    Education, a guide to reference and information sources /
Nancy Patricia O'Brien. -- 2nd ed.
        p.   cm. -- (Reference sources in the social sciences series)
    Rev. ed. of: Education, a guide to reference and information
sources / Lois J. Buttlar. 1989.
    Includes bibliographical references and indexes.
    ISBN 1-56308-626-3
    1. Education--Reference books Bibliography.   2. Education
Bibliography.   3. Social sciences--Reference books Bibliography.
4. Social sciences Bibliography.   I. Buttlar, Lois, 1934-
Education, a guide to reference and information sources.   II. Title.
III. Title: Education.   IV. Series.
Z5811.B89   1999
[LB15]
016.37--dc21   99-44764
                                                                    CIP

Dedicated to Dr. Yash Bhagwanji

*His commitment to improving the lives of
young children with special needs
serves as a shining example
of what education should and can be.*

CONTENTS

Introduction xi

1. General Education Sources 1
    Bibliographies 1
    Dictionaries and Encyclopedias 1
    Directories and Almanacs 6
    Guides, Handbooks, and Yearbooks 9
    Indexes and Abstracts 15
    Statistical Sources 19
    World Wide Web and Internet Sources 21
    Journals 23
    Biographies 33

2. Educational Technology and Media 37
    Dictionaries and Encyclopedias 37
    Directories and Almanacs 37
    Guides, Handbooks, and Yearbooks 38
    Journals 40

3. Early Childhood, Elementary, and Secondary Education . . . 45
    Dictionaries and Encyclopedias 45
    Directories and Almanacs 45
    Guides, Handbooks, and Yearbooks 48
    Statistical Sources 50
    Journals 51
    Biographies 54

4. Higher Education 55
    Bibliographies 55
    Dictionaries and Encyclopedias 55
    Directories and Almanacs 57
    Guides, Handbooks, and Yearbooks 66
    Indexes and Abstracts 70
    Statistical Sources 71
    World Wide Web and Internet Sources 73
    Journals 74

5. Multilingual and Multicultural Education **83**
Dictionaries and Encyclopedias 83
Directories and Almanacs 84
Guides, Handbooks, and Yearbooks 84
Statistical Sources 85
World Wide Web and Internet Sources 85
Journals 86

6. Special Education **91**
Dictionaries and Encyclopedias 91
Directories and Almanacs 92
Guides, Handbooks, and Yearbooks 93
Indexes and Abstracts 95
Journals 96

7. Adult, Alternative, Continuing, and Distance Education **105**
Dictionaries and Encyclopedias 105
Directories and Almanacs 106
Guides, Handbooks, and Yearbooks 107
World Wide Web and Internet Sources 108
Journals 108

8. Career and Vocational Education **111**
Directories and Almanacs 111
Guides, Handbooks, and Yearbooks 111
Journals 112

9. Comparative and International Education **115**
Dictionaries and Encyclopedias 115
Directories and Almanacs 116
Guides, Handbooks, and Yearbooks 117
Statistical Sources 118
Journals 119

10. Curriculum, Instruction, and Content Areas **123**
Dictionaries and Encyclopedias 123
Directories and Almanacs 124
Guides, Handbooks, and Yearbooks 125
Indexes and Abstracts 128
World Wide Web and Internet Sources 128
Journals 129

11. **Educational Administration and Management** **139**
  Guides, Handbooks, and Yearbooks 139
  Indexes and Abstracts 140
  Journals 140

12. **Educational History and Philosophy** **143**
  Dictionaries and Encyclopedias 143
  Directories and Almanacs 144
  World Wide Web and Internet Sources 145
  Journals 145
  Biographies 147

13. **Educational Research, Measurement, and Testing** **149**
  Dictionaries and Encyclopedias 149
  Directories and Almanacs 149
  Guides, Handbooks, and Yearbooks 152
  World Wide Web and Internet Sources 154
  Journals 154

14. **Educational Psychology** **161**
  Dictionaries and Encyclopedias 161
  Guides, Handbooks, and Yearbooks 162
  Journals 163

  Author Index 167
  Title Index 171
  Subject Index 181

INTRODUCTION

It is always a challenge to prepare the second edition of another individual's work. When a decade separates the two editions it becomes a matter of making major decisions about what is still relevant and what has become obsolete or outdated. Compiling the information in this guide has been a learning experience as I gathered sources and evaluated their effectiveness, and one that will be of benefit to library users. For example, the same day I discovered a slim volume of telecommunications numbers for distance programs among some gift materials, I was able to identify resources for a user half a continent away. Whether serendipity or synchronicity, such experiences highlighted the development of this guide and confirmed its usefulness to information seekers. I believe that those consulting this guide will find it equally helpful in identifying the best sources to satisfy information needs.

Scope and Purpose

The purpose of this guide is to provide information about the key reference and information resources in the field of education. The main audience for this guide is the community of information seekers and providers at libraries and schools that includes faculty, college and university students, librarians, and researchers. Other interested users are secondary school students looking for specific information sources, parents, school administrators, and the general public.

Sources in this guide include items published from 1990 through 1998. Selective inclusion of works published prior to 1990 occurred if the item was significant or unique. All items included are in English, although some are multilingual in content. Most publications are from the United States, the United Kingdom, Canada, Australia, and the Netherlands.

Many of the items included in the first edition of *Education: A Guide to Reference and Information Sources* (1989) by Lois A. Buttlar have been updated with more recent information. Most of the entries are new publications, however, or items not previously included. The first edition remains a useful complement because it retains bibliographies and other items of historical interest.

This guide includes many different types of information sources, but also excludes certain items and topic areas. Included are dictionaries, encyclopedias, directories, almanacs, guides, handbooks, yearbooks, indexing and abstracting services, statistical sources, Internet resources, and biographies. Excluded from this guide are lists of education associations and organizations. There are many comprehensive guides that provide this information and are updated regularly. For this type of information, the user should consult the *Encyclopedia of Associations* under headings for education; *EROD: Education Resource Organizations Directory* (see entry no. 65); or, the *Encyclopedia of Education Information* (see entry no. 23). Each of these directories will supply accessible, current information about educational associations and organizations, some of which may be available via the Internet as in the case of EROD.

Also excluded from this guide are reference and information sources for children's and young adult literature. *Children's Literature: A Guide to Information Sources*, 1998, by Margaret W. Denman-West provides an excellent resource for these materials.

Unlike the first edition, this guide does not include general social science reference and information sources. Those may be found in large part in Stephen H. Aby's *Sociology: A Guide to Reference and Information Sources* (1997). Again, it was felt that reproducing another author's efforts was not necessary when such thorough guides were already available.

Finally, one of the significant differences between the first and second edition of this guide is the type of material selected for inclusion. Not surprisingly, Internet sources are now included with URL address information. These were not even available when the first edition was published. While the first edition included many bibliographies, the present edition has very few. However, due to the increasing reliance on journals as a source of information, the number of journals listed in this guide is significant. While the quantity does not match the number listed in the *Current Index to Journals in Education*, which indexes over 950 journal titles, approximately 250 journals are included in this guide.

Selection Considerations

Books and handbooks published in 1990 or later are the focus of this guide in order to present current information sources. Unlike the first edition, few bibliographies were annotated because the ease of compiling customized bibliographies through electronic databases and catalogs has created a situation where users often develop their own databases and bibliographies of resources. This increased focus on accessibility to resources through electronic databases, particularly indexing and abstracting services, suggested that more journals should be included.

Of the universe of education-related journals that numbers over 1,000, a larger sample was selected for inclusion than appeared in the previous edition. The incorporation of nearly 250 journals reflects the reliance on these publications by educators, administrators, and researchers. From practical classroom magazines to intensely research-oriented journals, the demand for these publications is constant. Those included in this guide are either standard sources frequently consulted by students, educators, and researchers, or fill a very specialized information niche. When the information was readily available, reference to electronic versions of journals was incorporated. It is interesting to observe that the information supplied by the journal publishers varied greatly in accuracy. Several instances occurred when the journal indicated that it was indexed in publications that ceased several years ago, or that changed titles. A selected list of current education-related indexing or abstracting services is provided for journal entries.

Of particular note is the decision to include only selected guides to colleges and universities. A visit to any large bookstore will confirm that shelves of guides to the best programs for post-secondary study are available. Many of these guides have a particular focus on the needs of specialized populations, racial or ethnic groups, financial considerations, and so on. A representative sample of some of the better known directories such as the *College Blue Book* (see entry no. 174) or of those that have a particular focus such as the *Directory of College Facilities and Services for People with Disabilities* (see entry no. 274) are presented. Many other guides of varying quality are published and are available beyond those included here.

Organization

This guide is divided into fourteen categories that reflect different aspects of education. These categories are: general education sources; educational technology and media; early childhood, elementary, and secondary education; higher education; multilingual and multicultural education; special education; adult, alternative, continuing and distance education; career and vocational education; comparative and international education; curriculum, instruction, and content areas; educational administration and management; educational history and philosophy; educational research, measurement, and testing; and, educational psychology.

Each of these categories may have up to nine subcategories focusing on a different type of publication. These publication types include bibliographies; dictionaries and encyclopedias; directories and almanacs; guides, handbooks, and yearbooks; indexes and abstracts; statistical sources; World Wide Web and Internet sources; journals; and, biographies. Not all subcategories will appear within each subject category. Within each section entries are arranged alphabetically by author or editor and title.

Generally, the table of contents can be used to locate sources by subject and publication type, or to encourage browsing for relevant materials. Enhanced access by author, title and subject is provided through indexes. This should be particularly helpful with the section on curriculum, instruction, and the content areas where subject matter materials in areas such as science, mathematics, and the language arts are intermingled.

General Information

Entries follow the *Chicago Manual of Style* (14th ed.) format with descriptive annotations. Evaluative comments are included for many items. With the exception of two British indexing and abstracting publications, all sources were examined, reviewed, and annotated by the compiler. Publisher advertisements and familiarity with their other indexing and abstracting services were used as the basis for those two annotations.

Each entry includes the following information when available: author or editor, title, edition, place and date of publication, publisher, pagination or volumes, price, LC number, ISBN, series, and indexes. Prices for books and serials were taken from *Books in Print*, *Ulrich's International Periodicals Directory*, *EBSCO's Librarians Handbook*, from the items themselves, or publisher's catalogs. Journal prices are for institutional subscriptions. As is always the case, prices and availability are subject to change.

Acknowledgments

I would like to express my thanks to Ms. Kelly Ewalt for taking on the tedious task of verifying many of the journal and book prices found in this guide. Extensive appreciation is directed to series editor, Professor Robert Burger, for his patience and unwavering good humor as I worked with an unfamiliar software program. To those family, friends, and colleagues who bore with me during the development of this guide, I extend my heartfelt thanks. Any errors or omissions in this guide are my sole responsibility.

1

GENERAL EDUCATION SOURCES

Bibliographies

1. **Bibliographic Guide to Education 1998**. New York: G. K. Hall, 1999. 949 p. $385.00. ISSN: 0147-6505. ISBN: 0-7838-0209-9.

This annual guide lists recent publications in book, media and other formats that were cataloged by Teachers College, Columbia University. Contents are supplemented by recent items added to the Research Libraries of the New York Public Library. This guide is actually a massive bibliography of recently acquired or published material, excluding serials, in the field of education. Education at all levels and in all areas is covered, in both English and other languages. Arranged in a single alphabetical listing, each item is accessible by author, title, series title, and subject. Each item is listed with full information under the main entry, but with only brief information included under different access points. Useful for examining recent publications within the field of education.

Dictionaries and Encyclopedias

2. Anderson, Lorin W., ed. **International Encyclopedia of Teaching and Teacher Education**. 2nd ed. New York: Elsevier Science, 1995. 684 p. $196.50. LC: 95-45385. ISBN: 0-08042304-3.

Drawn from the second edition of the *International Encyclopedia of Education*, this work includes revisions to articles and new essays related to teaching and teacher education. Divided into two major segments, the one on teaching includes teacher characteristics; theories and models of teaching; instructional programs and strategies; teaching skills and techniques; school and classroom factors; students and the learning process; teaching for specific objectives; and, the study of teaching. The second segment on teacher education includes sections on concepts and issues in teacher education; generic initial teacher education; and continuing teacher education. Recognizing the conceptual shift in focus in education since the first edition was published in 1987, this edition incorporates a multidisciplinary perspective. Useful as an overview of teaching and teacher education, with well-referenced articles and suggestions for further reading. Subject and name indexes enhance access to the contents.

3.   Barrow, Robin, and Milburn, Geoffrey. **A Critical Dictionary of Educational Concepts: An Appraisal of Selected Ideas and Issues in Educational Theory and Practice**. 2nd ed. New York: Teachers College Press, 1990. 370 p. $45.00. LC: 90-36532. ISBN: 0-8077-3058-0.

The authors take an unabashed stance that the study of education is often done in a strictly scientific manner without taking other factors into consideration. Consequently their dictionary focuses on key concepts in educational theory and practice with the intent of creating a dialogue as to the impact of societal factors, philosophies, and current thought about these concepts. The generally lengthy entries are supported by an extensive bibliography. This dictionary is a useful counterpoint and supplement to more standard education dictionaries.

4.   Blake, David, and Hanley, Vincent. **The Dictionary of Educational Terms**. Brookfield, Vt.: Ashgate Publishing, 1995. 187 p. LC: 95-77012. ISBN: 1-85742-256-2.

Although this is a British publication, with definitions geared specifically to the National Curriculum in Great Britain, the terminology is also applicable more generally. Definitions are clear with cross-references that occasionally include addresses of relevant agencies or institutions for further information. They generally consist of a brief paragraph. A list of useful acronyms appears prior to the dictionary listings. This is a helpful guide to understanding British education and terminology.

5.   Dejnozka, Edward L., and Kapel, David E. **American Educator's Encyclopedia**. Rev. ed. Westport, Conn.: Greenwood Press, 1991. 716 p. $115.00. LC: 90-41510. ISBN: 0-313-25269-6. Revised edition by David E. Kapel, Charles S. Gifford, and Marilyn B. Kapel.

Approximately 2,000 entries related to terms and major figures in the field of education are included in this source. Each entry is relatively brief and defines the term or describes the organization, individual, or instrument in an easily understandable way. References are usually included with each entry, and often cross-references are provided as well. In addition to a lengthy index, appendixes that include information such as ethics codes, chronological listings of key government, association, and other educational leaders, and other useful information are provided. Excellent source of ready reference access to the key terms, events, and figures within the field of education.

6. Houston, James E., ed. **Thesaurus of ERIC Descriptors**. 13th ed. Phoenix, Ariz.: Oryx Press, 1995. 704 p. $69.50. ISSN: 1051-2993. ISBN: 0-89774-788-7.

The thirteenth edition of this indispensable resource includes 5,759 terms and 4,604 references for use with the Educational Resources Information Center (ERIC) database. Due to the extensive contents of the ERIC database, a controlled vocabulary is critical, and this guide provides a list of those vocabulary terms. Drawing upon the subject expertise of those who scan the education literature for inclusion in the ERIC database, new terms are added, and terms no longer current are relegated to cross-reference status. Brief scope notes or definitions are provided for many terms to place them in an educational context, with suggestions for broader, narrower, and related terms to use in an information search. The thesaurus is valuable not only as an aid for accurate and efficient searching of the ERIC database, but also as a limited glossary of educational terms. Also available electronically in conjunction with the ERIC database from selected vendors.

7. Houston, James E., Weller, Carolyn R., and Patt, Carol A., ed. **ERIC Identifier Authority List (IAL)**. Phoenix, Ariz.: Oryx Press, 1995. 591 p. $59.50. ISSN: 1062-0508. ISBN: 0-89774-890-5.

Published as a supplement to the *Thesaurus of ERIC Descriptors*, the identifier list provides additional terms that are used to index education literature in the ERIC database. Usually these terms are the names of projects, legislation, persons, places, organizations, tests, groups, or a new term that may eventually be elevated to descriptor status. Each identifier is listed with the number of occurrences in the ERIC print indexes. Identifiers are also listed separately in an alphabetical arrangement in categories indicating the type of identifier, such as person, legislation, or test. This is a useful tool for searching the ERIC database for topics such as "Head Start," which is an identifier not a descriptor.

8.   Husen, Torsten, and Postlethwaite, T. Neville, ed. **The International Encyclopedia of Education**. 2nd ed. Oxford, Eng.: Pergamon, 1994. 12 v. $3,902.00. LC: 94-3059. ISBN: 0-08-041046-4.

Over 1,200 entries written by authors from more than 95 countries are included in this international encyclopedia of education. Defining education in very broad terms, entries are divided into twenty-two major fields, and then subdivided into individual topics within those fields. Although entries are arranged alphabetically, the user should consult the thorough three-level subject index to locate relevant materials from other areas. Also provided are a name index, a classified list of entries, and a list of contributors. The editorial board is a prestigious group of internationally recognized educators, which has helped to insure a high quality encyclopedia. Also available as *Education: The Complete Encyclopedia (CD-ROM)* issued on the same CD-ROM with *Encyclopedia of Higher Education.*

9.   Lawton, Denis, and Gordon, Peter. **Dictionary of Education**. 2nd ed. London: Hodder & Stoughton, 1996. 250 p. ISBN: 0-340-64815-5.

More than a dictionary of education and training within the United Kingdom, this work contains four sections, each with a particular focus. The first section presents essays on the background of education and its key concepts. The second section is a dictionary with brief entries, and cross-references to other terms within this section as well as to concepts in the first section. The third section is a chronology of key events in the history of English education since 1800. The fourth and final section is a list of acronyms. A useful source of information about education in England and Wales for scholars and practitioners.

10.   McBrien, J. Lynn, and Brandt, Ronald S. **The Language of Learning: A Guide to Education Terms**. Alexandria, Va.: Association for Supervision and Curriculum Development, 1997. 114 p. $13.95. LC: 97-19649. ISBN: 0-87120-274-3.

This ASCD-sponsored glossary offers more than 200 education terms with definitions that range from three to four sentences to full page explanations. With a focus on K-12 education, the purpose of this book is to offer clear definitions of education terms for use by parents, the general public, policymakers, and others. Some entries include examples and resources (including World Wide Web sites) for further information. A topic list at the end of this slim publication provides a cross-listing of terms for additional information and exploration.

11. Noble, Keith Allan. **International Education Quotations Encyclo-paedia**. Buckingham, Eng.: Open University Press, 1995. 381 p. $50.00. LC: 94-36312. ISBN: 0-335-19394-3.

Drawing upon an international array of authors and historical figures, the quotations presented in this encyclopedia address all aspects of education. Containing nearly 2,700 entries from the ancient past to the present, it is possible to identify an apt quote for a particular use from this source. Arranged alphabetically, each educational concept or term has a single or several quotations attached to it. Quotes for "back to basics," "publish or perish," and many other ideas are presented. An index by authors is also included.

12. Palmer, James C., and Colby, Anita Y. **Dictionary of Educational Acronyms, Abbreviations, and Initialisms**. 2nd ed. Phoenix, Ariz.: Oryx Press, 1985. 97 p. $11.00. LC: 84-42814. ISBN: 0-89774-165-X.

This valuable guide to the proliferation of acronyms, abbreviations, and initialisms within education will aid the student, parent, educator, administrator or researcher searching for the meaning of a particular set of letters. In addition to an alphabetical listing of acronyms, a reverse listing by organization, program or institution name is also provided.

13. Saha, Lawrence J., ed. **International Encyclopedia of the Sociology of Education**. New York: Elsevier Science, 1997. 961 p. $266.50. LC: 97-24837. ISBN: 0-08-042990-4.

Drawn from the second edition of the *International Encyclopedia of Education*, this overview of the sociology of education includes revised and new articles. Addressing areas such as the social foundations of education, sociological theory, educational structures, and educational processes, the encyclopedia provides a framework for these topics within ten categories. The ten categories are social theories, sociological fields, research traditions, school as a social system, structure of educational systems, school processes, family and schooling, teachers in society, youth in schools, and educational policy and change. Contributors are prominent international educators and researchers who have provided extensive references for each chapter. Thorough subject and name indexes are included.

14. Shafritz, Jay M., Koeppe, Richard P., and Soper, Elizabeth W. **The Facts on File Dictionary of Education**. New York: Facts on File, 1988. 503 p. $145.70. LC: 88-24554. ISBN: 0-8160-1636-4.

One of the better known current education dictionaries, this Facts on File publication provides terminology that relates to preschool through high school education. In addition to general terms, entries for major education figures, court cases, selected journals, laws, organizations and well-known tests are included. Most entries are brief but some include more descriptive information as well as references. Reliable source of education terminology.

15.   Unger, Harlow G. **Encyclopedia of American Education**. New York: Facts on File, 1996. 3 vols. $175.00. LC: 95-41694. ISBN: 0-8160-2994-6.

With nearly 2,500 entries, the *Encyclopedia* covers most areas of education and provides additional references for further information. Major figures within the field of education, general terminology, and specific aspects of education are included in its three volumes. An extensive bibliography and list of references appears in volume 3, with its own subject guide or table of contents. Also in volume 3 are a chronology of major events within American education; a listing of significant federal legislation by date; a listing of major U.S. Supreme Court decisions affecting education; alphabetical lists of education degrees at the graduate level; and education and general majors available to undergraduate students within the United States. A lengthy and detailed index crowns this useful and thorough encyclopedia.

Directories and Almanacs

16.   Anderson, Beth, ed. **Directory of Curriculum Materials Centers**. 4th ed. Chicago: Association of College and Research Libraries, 1996. 165 p. $26.50. ISBN: 0-8389-7862-2

Published approximately every five years, the directory lists U.S. and Canadian curriculum materials centers at 278 institutions. Each center supports a teacher education program by housing representative preschool through high school instructional classroom materials. Arranged by state or province, each entry provides address, contact name, size of collection, and descriptive information. An appendix includes the data survey form, and an index provides a quick guide to the institutions represented.

17.   **Annual Register of Grant Support: A Directory of Funding Sources 1999**. 32nd ed. New Providence, N.J.: R. R. Bowker, 1998. 1,399 p. $199.95. LC: 69-18307. ISSN: 0066-4049. ISBN: 0-8352-4180-7.

Useful to scholars, researchers, practitioners and organizations, this directory lists sources of funding for a variety of purposes including study grants, grants for facilities, and research grants. Each funding agency is listed in a topical category such as humanities, special populations, physical sciences, technology and industry, and so on. A separate listing for multiple special purpose agencies is also included. Four indexes provide access by subject, organization and program, geographical location, and personnel. Entries typically include contact information, areas of interest, type of award, purpose, eligibility requirements, geographic restrictions, financial data, and application information. Useful source of funding information.

18. Butler, Gregory S., and Slack, James D. **U.S. Educational Policy Interest Groups: Institutional Profiles**. Westport, Conn.: Greenwood Press, 1994. 228 p. $75.00. LC: 93-44516. ISBN: 0-313-27292-1.

Listing 182 organizations that have an impact on educational policy, this directory provides not only basic demographic information about each organization (address, history, governance, funding) but also provides information about policy concerns and tactics and political activity. The source information was obtained through mail surveys, annual reports and other promotional literature, and through follow-up telephone queries. Entries are listed alphabetically, and appendixes provide supplemental information about government agencies concerned with education policy, legislative hearings, and the mail survey. The introduction provides background information about educational interest groups, some analysis of their level of political activity, and presents theories as to why such groups are not more active in lobbying. This is a unique directory of the political activities of education associations and organizations.

19. Cabell, David W. E., ed. **Cabell's Directory of Publishing Opportunities in Education**. 5th ed. Beaumont, Tex.: Cabell Publishing, 1998. 2 vols. $89.95. ISBN: 0-911753-12-5.

With over 440 education journals listed, Cabell's directory offers the budding or established author a list of potential journals in which to publish. Classified into twenty-seven subject areas, the journal entries provide all the basic information about the publisher, editor, address, review time, circulation, and price. Additional helpful information about acceptance rates and type of review process is included. Introductory matter on how the directory helps an author publish ideas has some very sound information about the manuscript submission process. A valuable aid to the potential author, and a useful guide to the education journal literature.

20. **Commonwealth Universities Yearbook. A Directory to the Universities of the Commonwealth and the Handbook of Their Associations**. 72nd ed. London: Association of Commonwealth Universities, 1996. 2 vol. $250.00. LC: 59-24175. ISSN: 0069-7745. ISBN: 0-85143-155-0.

With over 600 entries reflecting the many institutions of higher learning represented in the Commonwealth, this directory provides current information about university systems in each country, and address, telephone, e-mail and FAX numbers of academic departments, as well as names of faculty and administrators. Profiles of inter-university organizations with constituents from the Commonwealth universities are featured for the first time in the 72nd edition. The handbook of the Association of Commonwealth Universities is provided in the front matter. An extensive index by personal name and an institution index are provided in volume 2. Excellent resource for information about Commonwealth universities.

21. **Directory of Public School Systems in the United States 1997-98**. 23rd ed. Evanston, Ill.: American Association for Employment in Education, Inc., 1997. 198 p. $70.00 (nonmembers); $40.00 (members).

Annually updated directory of school districts in the U.S. arranged by state and city. In addition to contact name, address and telephone information, World Wide Web addresses are provided when available. Codes provide data about grade levels and enrollment. Each entry also indicates the last time the data was verified. A listing of state teacher certification offices and addresses is provided.

22. **Directory of State Education Agencies**. 11th ed. Washington, D.C.: Council of Chief State School Officers, 1994. 113 p. $22.00. ISSN: 0897-4462.

A concise directory from the Council of Chief State School Officers (CCSSO) that provides listings of all state education agencies and key staff, vocational education agencies, a table of state education governance indicating elected or appointed boards, relevant national associations, CCSSO officers, staff and agency networks, and an organizational directory of the U.S. Department of Education. Address and phone numbers are included in each category. Due to the rapid turnover in government circles, this directory provides key information that may still require verification through follow-up contact.

23. Mackenzie, Leslie, ed. **Encyclopedia of Education Information, 1997**. 2nd ed. Lakeville, Ct.: Grey House Publishing, 1996. 537 p. $156.25. ISBN: 0-939300-74-5.

This directory provides access to education associations, organizations, and government agencies. Relevant conferences and trade shows are also listed as are education databases, directories, research centers, employment resources, grants, fundraising and financial aid opportunities, information on school libraries, journals and newsletters, publishers of educational materials and media, suppliers, and state statistics. Each entry includes contact information and generally includes brief descriptive information. Useful as a quick guide to sources of education information. Also available electronically. Includes entry/title, publisher, and subject indexes. The forthcoming 1999/2000 edition has a new title, *Educators Resource Directory*, which more accurately reflects the purpose and focus.

24. Silvey, Marvin W., and Silvey, Merrill H, ed. **Master's Theses Directories**. Cedar Falls, Iowa: Master's Theses Directories, 1997. 463 p. ISSN: 1072-5903.

   Published since 1952, this directory to research published as master's theses provides access to theses in the fields of education, arts and social sciences, and natural and technical sciences. Only those theses that are available for interlibrary loan are included because of the editor's concern that research information is to be shared, and not isolated at a single institution. Arrangement is by subject area, subdiscipline, and then alphabetically by author. Subject, author, and institution indexes provide additional points of access. A bibliography of further sources to consult for master's theses is appended. Formerly issued as *Master's Theses in Education*. Useful source of information for research at the master's level.

Guides, Handbooks, and Yearbooks

25. Berry, Dorothea M. **A Bibliographic Guide to Educational Research**. 3rd ed. Metuchen, N.J.: Scarecrow Press, 1990. 500 p. $55.00. LC: 90-48184. ISBN: 0-8108-2343-8.

   This guide offers descriptive listings of materials useful to the scholar or researcher seeking education information. It is divided into categories such as books, periodicals, research studies, government publications, special types of literature, other types of reference materials, and sources for writing a research paper. Although most materials included are from the 1980s, the listings are still generally useful. Some limited guidance on conducting educational research is included.

26. Biddle, Bruce J., Good, Thomas L., and Goodson, Ivor F., ed. **International Handbook of Teachers and Teaching**. Dordrecht, The Netherlands: Kluwer Academic, 1997. 2 vol., 1,474 p. (*Kluwer International Handbooks of Education* v. 3). ISBN: 0-7923-3532-5.

   In two volumes, the recent research on teachers and teaching is presented through a series of chapters written by some of the major figures in the field. The evolving role of teachers is explored in relation to multiculturalism, feminism, professionalization, reform projects, students, social and political contexts, and more. Well referenced, and well indexed, this is an impressive compilation of the state of teaching and teachers across cultural and geopolitical lines.

27. Brown, David. **Information Sources for Teachers**. Brookfield, Vt.: Ashgate, 1996. 328 p. $49.95. LC: 96-85392. ISBN: 1-85742-231-7.

Useful if unpretentious directory of agencies, organizations, and local education authorities in the United Kingdom. Lacking a preface or introduction, this directory provides five categories of resource information: administration, curriculum, students, teachers, and parents. National as well as local agencies are listed under administration. Curriculum includes everything from subject areas to school tour operators. Support and other relevant groups are listed under teachers, students, and parents. Each entry provides an address and a brief description of the organization's purpose. Subject and organization indexes are provided.

28. Clarke, Peter B. **Finding Out in Education: A Guide to Sources of Information**. 2nd ed. Harlow, Essex, Eng.: Longman, 1993. 228 p. ISBN: 0-582-21797-0.

This guide to the education literature has a primarily British and Scottish focus, with inclusion of other relevant European and American sources. In addition to listing key reference tools in education with annotations, selected general sources have been provided as well to assist the general library researcher. Some monographic publications have been included, often without annotations, as further resources within the various categories: dictionaries, yearbooks, official publications, education law, bibliographies, and so on. Title and subject indexes provide additional access points. Useful source for British and European educational materials.

29. Cummings, William K., and McGinn, Noel F., ed. **International Handbook of Education and Development: Preparing Schools, Students and Nations for the Twenty-First Century**. New York: Elsevier Science, 1997. 907 p. $128.50. ISBN: 0-08-0430678.

Contributions from prominent international educators are included in this ambitious handbook that chronicles the interrelated impact of education and society in its 49 chapters. Broadly, the chapters address the development and spread of the modern school; general issues in educational reform; issues within specific countries; the evolving relationship between development and education; environmental, political, community, and economic factors in education; and alternatives and innovations to educational practice. A slim subject index is provided in addition to an author index.

30. Entwistle, Noel, ed. **Handbook of Educational Ideas and Practices**. London: Routledge, 1990. 1,140 p. $150.00. LC: 89-10482. ISBN: 0-415-02061-1.

   The authors of the 101 chapters in this massive handbook are drawn primarily from the United Kingdom. Nevertheless, the topics addressed are global in nature and not restricted to a single geographical area or educational system. Chapters are organized within nine areas dealing with recurrent issues; education in contrasting societies; education beyond school; organization and management; curriculum design and evaluation; learning and teaching; teaching and assessment techniques; individual differences and development; and special educational needs. Suitably lengthy subject and name indexes are provided in this compendium of practices, theories and research in education.

31. Farrell, Michael, Kerry, Trevor, and Kerry, Carolle. **Blackwell Handbook of Education**. Oxford, Eng.: Blackwell, 1995. 333 p. LC: 94-27461. ISBN: 0-631-19279-4.

   The handbook is divided into four sections. The first is an alphabetical list of entries in dictionary and sometimes encyclopedic format. This section often provides a brief explanation of terminology relevant to education in Great Britain, and nearly as frequently the explanation expands to include an overview, cross-references, and further readings. The second section contains a list of acronyms and abbreviations, the third contains a directory of British and Welsh organizations, and the fourth provides a chronological series of descriptions of education legislation in England and Wales from 1861 to 1980. A classified list of entries in eight categories serves as both a key and an index to handbook topics. Useful for education research about the United Kingdom.

32. Freed, Melvyn N., Hess, Robert K., and Ryan, Joseph M. **Educator's Desk Reference (EDR): A Sourcebook of Educational Information and Research**. New York: Macmillan, 1989. 536 p. (*American Council on Education/Macmillan Series on Higher Education*). $49.95. LC: 88-9249. ISBN: 0-02-910740-7.

   Despite the fact that this resource is now somewhat dated, it still provides a useful guide to locating information and undertaking educational research. Information sources by type of publication (dictionary, yearbook, and so on), a guide to appropriate reference sources in education, education journals, publishers of education books, microcomputer software publishers, software for educational research, standardized tests, research processes, and selected educational organizations are described in this reference resource. A lengthy section is devoted to the research process and, in its 130 pages, introduces the researcher to linking research questions to design and statistical procedures, sampling techniques, and offers a research process checklist. An index provides access to the contents by title, organization name, topic, and research process in a single alphabetical listing.

33. Gough, Jeanne. ed. **Education Sourcebook**. Detroit, Mich.: Omnigraphics, 1997. 1,123 p. (*Personal Concerns Series* v. 1). $72.00. LC: 96-38291. ISBN: 0-7808-0179-2. "Basic Information About National Education Expectations and Goals, Including School Readiness, High School Completion, Adult Education, How Parents Can Help Ready Their Children for School, Along with Reports and Programs on Learning Disabilities, Students at Risk, National Excellence, How to Prepare for College, and How to Return to Education." (from title page and cover)

The *Sourcebook* consists of articles culled primarily from federal agencies. Divided into four sections, Educational Expectations, Helping Your Child Prepare for School, Issues and Concerns in Education, and Adult Education and Literacy, this book is geared toward answering the information needs of the general public. Current topics of interest, particularly those related to education standards, school reform, school readiness, and literacy are covered. Appendixes provide references for further reading from two major areas of interest: at risk students and readiness goals. Useful compilation, particularly for the public and libraries without access to federal documents.

34. Hargreaves, Andy, Lieberman, Ann, Fullan, Michael, and Hopkins, David. ed. **International Handbook of Educational Change**. Dordrecht, The Netherlands: Kluwer Academic, 1998. 2 vols., 1,366 p. (*Kluwer International Handbooks of Education*). $395.00. LC: 97-051861. ISBN: 0-7923-3534-1.

This two-volume handbook features some of the major writers and researchers in the field of educational change and reform. Chapters address and analyze the educational change process as well as practices. Differing perspectives are represented. The framework is in four sections: Roots of Educational Change, Extending Educational Change, Fundamental Change, and The Practice and Theory of School Improvement. As a historical overview of educational change and an analysis of its current state, this handbook offers a valuable compilation of informative essays in a single source.

35. Holmes, Patricia A., and Rahn, Mikala L. **Resource Guide to Educational Standards**. http://ncrve.berkeley.edu/MDS-1205/. Berkeley, Calif.: National Center for Research in Vocational Education, 1998. 18 p. $3.25.

    Citing the ongoing interest and concern related to educational reform, this publication addresses the development of standards to improve and monitor reform efforts. Special emphasis is given to systemic reform efforts. Chapters list industry skill standards, academic skill standards, other standards resources, standards for teachers, vocational student organizations, and a bibliography. Web addresses are included with almost every entry. Slim but useful compilation of standards information, particularly related to academic and vocational areas.

36. Klein, Barry, ed. **Guide to American Educational Directories**. 7th ed. West Nyack, N.Y.: Todd Publications, 1994. 353 p. $75.00. ISBN: 0-915344-29-7.

    This "directory of directories" covers everything from professional association membership directories to directories of business suppliers to school and college directories. Impressive compilation of thousands of directories provides brief descriptions, full publisher addresses including telephone numbers, and prices for each entry. The directory is arranged topically from accounting to zoological sciences, all with an education-related focus. Category and title indexes provide quick access to directories.

37. Loke, Wing Hong. **A Guide to Journals in Psychology and Education**. Metuchen, N.J.: Scarecrow Press, 1990. 410 p. $44.00. LC: 90-33603. ISBN: 0-8108-2327-6.

    Of interest to authors planning to submit manuscripts and to those seeking information about psychology and education journals, this guide offers detailed information about submission requirements. Although dated in several areas, the list of journals is still useful as are the submission details. Subscription costs are no longer current, and the editor information is most likely outdated. However, the information about the submission process including whether it is a refereed journal, acceptance criteria, acceptance rate, consideration time, and publication lag remains quite useful. Similarly the information regarding the focus, special features, article content and readership of each journal is still valuable. Useful addition to a general education and/or psychology collection.

38. **Making Standards Matter: An Annual Fifty-State Report on Efforts to Raise Academic Standards**. Washington, D.C.: American Federation of Teachers, 1995-. $10.00.

Issued annually since 1995, this AFT publication presents and analyzes the status of academic standards in the United States. Divided into five sections, the report provides easily understandable assessments of each state's progress in improving academic standards. Section one describes AFT's criteria for judging state reforms. Section two presents an overview of the situation. Section three makes recommendations about improving reform efforts. Section four outlines each state's current situation regarding standards, and section five reproduces the responses from each state's education department. Unique and useful guide to educational reform and academic standards in the U.S.

39. Mastain, Richard K., ed. **NASDTEC Manual 1991: Manual on Certification and Preparation of Educational Personnel in the United States**. Dubuque, Iowa: Kendall/Hunt Publishing, 1991. 1 vol.; various pagings. $69.95. ISBN: 0-8403-7104-7.

Published on behalf of the National Association of State Directors of Teacher Education and Certification, and based upon a 220 page questionnaire sent to each state's licensing agency, this compilation provides detailed information regarding certification issues. Divided into 17 sections, each with its own paging, the manual includes information on standard certification, emergency certificates, out-of-state certification, and alternative teacher certification. Certification requirements for Department of Defense Dependents Schools and the Canadian provinces are included. A list of tables provides some subject access but does not overcome the lack of an index. This is nonetheless a valuable guide to certification practices and issues across the states.

40. National Society for the Study of Education. **Yearbook**. 97th ed. Chicago: National Society for the Study of Education (NSSE), 1998. 2 vols. $56.00. ISSN: 0077-5762.

The yearbook of NSSE is issued annually in two volumes, each having its own thematic focus. Highly regarded, and published since 1895, each volume offers a serious and thoughtful review of educational issues. Authors of the several chapters in each yearbook are drawn from scholars and practitioners who are active in their respective fields. Valuable resource for capturing current key topics in education.

41.   **NEA Handbook 1995-1996**. Washington, D.C.: National Education Association, 1995. 480 p. $15.95. ISSN: 8755-1829.

The annual publication of the National Education Association's handbook provides NEA with the opportunity to briefly review the current state of American education before moving into a description of the governance structure, committees, affiliates, policy documents, selected history, and other information of interest to members and the general education community. The mission statement and code of ethics are also provided, as are subject and name indexes.

42.   Sikula, John, Buttery, Thomas J., and Guyton, Edith, ed. **Handbook of Research on Teacher Education**. 2nd ed. New York: Macmillan, 1996. 1,190 p. $75.00. LC: 95-7504. ISBN: 0-02-897194-9.

Extensively referenced articles on the theory and practice of teacher education are presented in the second edition of this handbook, which is a project of the Association of Teacher Educators. Articles appear in seven categories addressing teacher education as a field of study; recruitment, selection and initial preparation; contextual influences; curriculum; continuing professional growth, development, and assessment; diversity and equity issues; and new and emerging directions. Lengthy author and subject indexes provide multiple access points to the contents of the handbook. A rich and significant source of research on teacher education.

Indexes and Abstracts

43.   **Australian Education Index**. Melbourne, Vict.: Australian Council for Educational Research, 1958 -. v. 40, 1997. Issued quarterly with an annual cumulation. $195.00 (Australia); $270.00 (overseas). ISSN: 0004-9026.

Provides references and abstracts to Australian education literature published in journal articles, monographs, conference papers, government reports, research reports, and curriculum documents. Also included are articles and reports by Australian authors or about Australian education published overseas. Subject terms are taken from the *Australian Thesaurus of Education Descriptors*. The list of subject terms is extensive and thorough, and is supplemented by an author and institution index. Also available electronically.

44.   **Canadian Education Index/Repertoire Canadien Sur l'Education**. Toronto, Ont.: Micromedia Ltd., 1965-. v. 32, 1997. Issued quarterly with an annual cumulation. $368.00. ISSN: 0008-3453.

Provides references and abstracts to Canadian education literature published in journal articles, monographs, dissertations and theses, government reports, research reports, curriculum documents, and forthcoming titles. Government reports include publications from federal, provincial, and territorial departments. An extensive subject index in both English and French provides added value to the index, as do the corporate and personal name indexes and list of series titles. The *Canadian Education Thesaurus* is used as the basis for the subject terminology. Also available electronically.

45. **Contents Pages in Education**. Vol. 1-. Abingdon, Oxfordshire, Eng.: Carfax, 1986-. monthly. $880.00. ISSN: 0265-9220.

Over 700 international journals in education are included in this service. Contents pages of these journals are presented in alphabetical order by the title of the journal. Also includes author and subject indexes, a list of the journals included in each monthly issue, a list of all journals included in the service, and a list of new titles added. As a current awareness service, this publication provides regular access to the contents of journals published within education. Although somewhat different in purpose, this publication should be compared to indexing and abstracting services in order to verify that it will fill an existing gap in services.

46. **Current Index to Journals in Education (CIJE)**. Phoenix, Ariz.: Oryx Press, 1969-. v. 30, 1998. monthly. $245.00. ISSN: 0011-3565.

Monthly index and abstracting service that covers over 950 journals in education and its related disciplines. A list of the source journals, including publication information and some indication of how comprehensively each journal is indexed, is provided. Author and subject indexes, as well as a journal (table of) contents index are included. Subject terms follow those used in the *Thesaurus of ERIC Descriptors*, and additions and changes to thesaurus terms are included in each monthly index. Also available electronically through several vendors as part of the ERIC system.

47. **Education Index**. New York: H. W. Wilson, 1929-. v. 69, 1998. 10 issues per year. $280 minimum; determined by subscriber's periodical holdings. ISSN: 0013-1385.

Issued ten times per year, this index follows the standard pattern of alphabetical entries for subject and author in a single list. No abstracts are provided. Periodicals, yearbooks, and monographs are included as are reviews of videotapes, motion pictures, and computer programs. Book reviews are included in a separate listing at the end of each issue. Approximately 400 periodicals in the field of education and its related disciplines are indexed, and listed separately with publisher information. There is significant overlap with *Current Index to*

Journals in Education, except for the yearbooks indexed. Also available electronically from the publisher.

48. **International Bulletin of Bibliography on Education**. Madrid, Spain: International Bulletin of Bibliography on Education, 1982-. Issued bimonthly, with an annual number. $352.00. ISSN: 0211-8335.

    Issued in six languages (English, French, German, Italian, Portuguese, and Spanish), this index provides access to education literature in a truly international manner. Using the Universal Decimal Classification system, it is possible to identify categories of materials in broad subject and geographic areas by means of the classification number. Technical assistance in preparation of this index was provided by UNESCO and the International Bureau of Education, and reflects the inclusion of materials published in countries around the globe. Due to the complexity of the classification and subject scheme used, and the focus on international education, this index is best located in a research setting with regular demand for international resources.

49. **Linguistics and Language Behavior Abstracts**. Vol. 1-. San Diego, Calif.: Sociological Abstracts, Inc., 1967-. 5 issues per year. $405.00 (institutions). ISSN: 0888-8027.

    This abstracting service covers language behavior, linguistics, and related disciplines including the teaching of languages, second language learning, and other education-related topics. Special education issues arc also addressed. Formerly *Language and Language Behavior Abstracts,* and also known as *LLBA*. Incorporates *Reading Abstracts*. An annual cumulative index is published separately. Also available electronically.

50. **Resources in Education (RIE)**. Washington, D.C.: U.S. Government Printing Office, 1975-. v. 33, 1998. $88.00; $415.00 annual cumulation. ISSN: 0098-0897. Volumes 1-9, 1966-1974 published as *Research in Education*. An annual cumulation is published by Oryx Press and available as a separate subscription.

    Monthly abstracting service that covers recent report literature in the field of education and related disciplines. Reports are from a variety of agencies, associations, and individuals, and many are reproduced on microfiche and available for purchase. In addition to abstracts of each report, separate indexes to subjects, authors, institutions/sponsoring agencies, publication types, and cross-references to ERIC clearinghouse numbers are provided. As part of the ERIC system, RIE provides access to education literature that otherwise would be difficult to track down. Uses the *Thesaurus of ERIC Descriptors* as the basis for subject indexing. Available electronically from several vendors as part of the ERIC database.

51.   Sheffield, Phil. ed. **British Education Index**. Leeds, Eng.: University of Leeds, 1954-. v. 34, 1998. $278.00. ISSN: 0007-0637. Earlier volumes published as *Index to Selected British Educational Periodicals*.

Quarterly index of educational articles published in the British Isles, and selected internationally published journals. Standard index information is provided without abstracts. Separate author and subject lists provide full citations of articles. A list of periodicals indexed is also included. Subject terms are taken from the *British Education Thesaurus*. Useful source of information about British educational practices and research. Annual print cumulative index provided as part of subscription. Also available electronically.

52.   **Sociology of Education Abstracts**. Vol. 1-. Abingdon, Oxfordshire, Eng.: Carfax, 1965-. quarterly. $634.00 (institutions). ISSN: 0038-0415.

Journals, books, and related literature are abstracted in this source covering the sociology of education. While international in focus, there is a strong emphasis on materials published in the United Kingdom. Sources on the research, teaching, and study of education and its role within society are included. Useful abstracting service for specialized collections of education, particularly those with a higher education and research focus.

53.   **State Education Journal Index, and Educators' Guide to Periodicals Research Strategies**. Westminster, Colo.: State Education Journal Index, 1963-. v. 34, July 1996-June 1997. annual. $79.00 yr. ISSN: 0039-0046.

As the title indicates, this index covers journals and periodicals in education that address current issues within American states. Journals indexed are usually not included in more traditional indexes, and in fact are often newsletters, state education association journals, and state school board association journals. Issued annually in August, the index provides access to literature that is often difficult to identify, but unfortunately, the articles and issues are often out-of-date by the time the annual publication appears. An introductory section on how to undertake research in the education journal literature is very helpful. A cross-referenced list of subject categories provides easy access to the contents of the index.

Statistical Sources

54. **Condition of Teaching: A State-by-State Analysis, 1990**. Princeton, N.J.: Carnegie Foundation for the Advancement of Teaching, 1990. 330 p. $12.00. ISSN: 1053-0053. ISBN: 0-931050-39-1.

Based on a survey of teacher opinions of education, this report includes highlights of the survey responses and state-by-state comparisons. Survey categories include teacher attitudes and values; student issues; learning and instruction; school climate; school facilities and materials; teacher involvement in decision making; status of the profession; and achieving excellence. The tables are supplemented by a narrative summary in the section on survey highlights. Similar to a public opinion poll, this report provides a good sense of the current state and the concerns of the teaching profession.

55. Halstead, Kent. **Three R's: Race Retention Rates by State**. Washington, D.C.: Research Associates of Washington, 1994. 33 p. $20.00. ISSN: 1077-7180.

In compact format, this statistical compilation of retention rates of different racial groups by state includes an introductory overview and analysis. Weighted scores are provided for securing a high school diploma, entering college, and college graduation. Based on the data and information gathered, each state is ranked for retention of its different racial populations. Interesting and informative compilation of student educational attainment by race.

56. Hattendorf Westney, Lynn C., ed. **Educational Rankings Annual 1999**. Detroit: Gale, 1998. 730 p. $190.00. ISSN: 0077-4472. ISBN: 0-7876-1187-5.

Compiled from educational and other published sources, these rankings address reputation, faculty publications, faculty salaries, tuition rates, test scores, alumni achievement, admissions selectivity, and other topics about the quality of education at all levels. Using selected sources considered to be of high quality and reputable, the editor has compiled an array of statistics and other information with the source listed in each instance, the number of entries in the ranking, and brief criteria used for rankings. Approximately 3,700 rankings and lists are provided. An extensive index includes topics as well as institutions being ranked. Valuable, popular, and reputable source of rankings information.

57. **Rankings of the States 1995**. Washington, D.C.: National Education Association (NEA), 1995. 59 p.

The state rankings data provided in this NEA publication is drawn from the federal government and other sources. The information provided on public education can be used in comparisons between states, to determine trends, and to evaluate progress. Statistics include population; enrollment, attendance, and membership; faculty; financial resources; government revenue; school revenue; government expenditures; and school expenditures. A bibliography, glossary, index, and supplemental information about special state situations are included.

58.   U.S. Department of Education. National Center for Education Statistics. **Digest of Education Statistics**. http://www.ed.gov/NCES/pubs/D96/. Washington, D.C.: U.S. Department of Education, 1996. 523 p. $44.00.

Regarded as the primary source of statistical information about American education, this source covers kindergarten through graduate education. Using both private and government sources of data, tabulations include enrollments, graduates, numbers of teachers, schools and colleges, educational attainment, funding, and population demographics. The focus is on national statistics, generally subdivided by population characteristics such as age, gender or race, or by geographic divisions. The National Center for Education Statistics is the primary source of data, but each table identifies the source and currency of information.

59.   U.S. Department of Education. National Center for Education Statistics. **The Condition of Education**. http: //www.ed.gov/NCES/pubs/ce/. Washington, D.C.: U.S. Department of Education, 1997. 411 p. $25.00.

Federal law mandates an annual statistical report on the condition and progress of education in the U.S. and other countries in order to promote and improve American education. This compilation and analysis meets that mandate. Using indicators as a mechanism for monitoring developments in education, this work introduces each section with an overview and discussion followed by the indicators over a varying span of years. A supplemental volume, *The Condition of Education 1997 Supplemental and Standard Error Tables*, is also available for further information. Each year different topics are chosen for in-depth discussion. Clear attribution to original sources of data is provided. The language is accessible to the general public, and the content of interest to anyone concerned about education.

World Wide Web and Internet Sources

60. **American School Directory (ASD)**. http://www.asd.com/asd/ asdhome.htm (accessed February 26, 1999).

    With more than 70,000 school sites included in the database, it is easy to locate the address and Web site for a particular private or public U.S. school. Each site has options for calendars, alumni directories, and more. While dependent on contributions from the schools and their alumni for some information, this is sure to develop into an easy way to trace alumni through a single source, as well as provide quick information about each school. The school information section supplies everything from school colors to names and telephone numbers for administrative personnel. Useful in its current form, this directory will improve with increased information.

61. **Chinese Educational Resources Information Centre Project (Chinese ERIC)**. http://www1.fed.cuhk.edu.hk/en/index.htm (accessed February 28, 1999).

    Developed as a free electronic database of educational studies in Chinese communities, this site mirrors the ERIC database with indexing of selected education journals and use of a thesaurus of education terminology. The database contains approximately 8,000 entries with over 2,700 including abstracts. The contents include English and Chinese articles published in 17 leading educational journals in Hong Kong, the Chinese Mainland and Taiwan dating back to 1990, and educational theses or dissertations dating back to 1980. Useful and expanding source of specialized information about Chinese education.

62. **Developing Educational Standards**. http://putwest.boces. org/Standards.html (accessed February 28, 1999).

    One of the advantages of this Web site, which lists standards, is that it provides information about the source of the standards, such as national organizations, state agencies, and others. Included on this site is information about educational standards and curriculum frameworks from national, state, local, and other Internet sources. Standards are arranged by state, subject area, U.S. government, other countries, and organizations. Developed and maintained by the Putnam Valley Central Schools, New York, this site offers a major service to anyone seeking information about standards, their development, and the actual text.

63. **Education Virtual Library**. http: //www.csu.edu.au/education/ library.html (accessed February 28, 1999).

A huge number of links to education sites around the world are presented at this site. Access can be made alphabetically by site, education level, type of resources provided, type of site, and by country. Education is often used in the broadest sense, and many of the sites are commercial so some caution may be needed in scrolling through this resource. A search feature is offered so that access to specific topics, services and resources is provided. Potentially useful site to massive amounts of education resources.

64. **Educational Information Resources Information Center: ERIC**. http://www.accesseric.org:81/ (accessed February 28, 1999).

This gateway to the ERIC system is presented by the National Library of Education. Descriptions of ERIC sites, access to ERIC publications and other resources, lists of ERIC listservs with subscription information, conference calendars, and general information about the ERIC system are provided. This is a rich source of information about ERIC with links to relevant sponsoring government entities, such as the National Library of Education and the U.S. Department of Education.

65. **EROD: Education Resource Organizations Directory**. http://www.ed.gov/BASISDB/EROD/direct/SF (accessed December 14, 1998).

Developed as an electronic directory of organizations that provide assistance and information on education-related topics, this site offers searching at simple and advanced levels as well as by state or territory. It also encourages the submission of new organizations or updating of outdated information via electronic forms. A descriptive page outlines how the site may be used by different audiences, the types of organizations included, and the fields of information provided in each entry. An icon regularly appears as a help feature to guide the searcher through this Web directory. Regular updates greatly increase its value.

66. **National Assessment of Educational Progress**.   http://nces.ed.gov/nationsreportcard/ (accessed February 27, 1999).

The National Assessment of Educational Progress (NAEP) has a congressional mandate to continuously assess the knowledge, skills, and performance of the nation's children and youth. NAEP provides objective data about student performance in the areas of reading, mathematics, science and writing at national, regional, and, on a trial basis, state levels. This information is now available electronically through the NAEP Web site. Other areas that have been assessed include citizenship, U.S. history, geography, social studies, art, music, literature, computer competence, career and occupational development, health, energy, consumer mathematics, and young adult literacy. Data about the school, administrators, and teachers are also routinely collected and reported. National reports, state reports, summary reports and more are available through this statistical Web site.

67. **National Public School Locator**. http://nces.ed.gov/ccdweb/school/school.asp (accessed February 27, 1999).

This locator provides the name, address, phone number, and other characteristics of a public school or school district when only limited information is known by the requester. Supported by the National Center for Education Statistics (NCES), the site features a search service to locate information. The information is drawn from recent NCES data surveys. Enrollment figures by grade, racial and ethnic populations, student-teacher ratio, number of teachers, and type of school are typically indicated for each school or district. Useful source of statistical and location information for U.S. schools.

68. **U.S. Department of Education (ED) Home Page**. http://www.ed.gov/ (accessed February 26, 1999).

Information by and about the U.S. Department of Education is supplied on this Web site. From popular sources of financial aid information (including forms) to education statistics, this is a comprehensive source of information from the U.S. Department of Education. Reports, programs and services, funding opportunities, and Department personnel are all listed on this site. The list of other electronic education resources is particularly useful. This is an extensive site with regular updates.

Journals

69. **American Educator**. Vol. 1-. Washington, D.C.: American Federation of Teachers, AFL-CIO, 1977-. quarterly. $8.00 (nonmembers). ISSN: 0148-423X.

Practical and inspirational articles abound in this mouthpiece of the AFT. As a guide to hands-on ways in which to improve classroom activities, this journal fulfills its mission. Indexed in: *Current Index to Journals in Education, Education Index.*

70. **American Journal of Education**. Vol. 1-. Chicago: University of Chicago Press, 1893-. quarterly. $77.00 (institutions). ISSN: 0195-6744.

Formerly *School Review.* Bridging the span between research, theory and implementation, this journal addresses all areas of education, particularly as they relate to policy, practice, and philosophy. Also includes book reviews. Indexed in: *Current Index to Journals in Education, Education Index, Social Sciences Citation Index, Sociology of Education Abstracts.*

71. **American School Board Journal**. Vol. 1-. Alexandria, Va.: National School Boards Association, 1891-. monthly. $54.00 (institutions). ISSN: 0003-0953.

Directed to school boards, this journal contains features useful to school administrators as well. Current issues related to school management are explored, and regular features include book reviews, legislative updates, and ERIC-provided summaries of feature articles. Indexed in: *Current Index to Journals in Education, Education Index, Educational Administration Abstracts.*

72. **American School & University**. Vol. 1-. Overland Park, Kans.: PRIMEDIA Intertec, 1928-. monthly. $50.00 (institutions). ISSN: 0003-0945.

Practical source of information for school and university facilities, business and purchasing issues, and life safety resources. Extensive classified advertising is included. Indexed in: *Current Index to Journals in Education, Education Index.*

73. **British Journal of Educational Studies**. Vol. 1-. Malden, Mass.: Blackwell, 1952-. quarterly. $269.00 (institutions). ISSN: 0007-1005.

For the researcher interested in the state of British education, this journal addresses both current and historical trends and issues. Strong emphasis is given to policy issues within the United Kingdom. Indexed in: *British Education Index, Education Index, Educational Administration Abstracts, Multicultural Education Abstracts, Research into Higher Education Abstracts, Sociology of Education Abstracts.*

74. **British Journal of Sociology of Education**. Vol. 1-. Abingdon, Oxfordshire, Eng.: Carfax, 1980-. quarterly. $598.00. ISSN: 0142-5692.

This refereed journal contains theoretical and empirical research articles related to sociology of education. In addition, extended reviews and review essays also appear in most issues. International in scope, a predominance of contributors are from Europe and the Antipodes. Indexed in: *British Education Index,*

Current Index to Journals in Education, Multicultural Education Abstracts, Social Sciences Citation Index, Sociology of Education Abstracts.

75. **Canadian Journal of Education/Revue Canadienne de l'education**. Vol. 1-. Ottawa, Ont., Canada: Canadian Society for the Study of Education, 1976-. quarterly. $100.00. ISSN: 0380-2361.

Articles in both English and French appear in this journal devoted to issues and problems in Canadian education. Research articles, brief research reports, and book reviews comprise the majority of each issue. These may be supplemented by essay reviews and discussion notes. Indexed in: *Canadian Education Index, Current Index to Journals in Education, Education Index, Sociology of Education Abstracts.*

76. **Contemporary Education**. Vol. 1-. Terra Haute, Ind.: School of Education, Indiana State University, 1930-. quarterly. $16.00. ISSN: 0010-7476.

Offers a forum for discussions of current problems in education. Brief research reports, short articles, and book reviews are included in each issue. All levels of education are considered, although the focus is elementary and secondary education. Indexed in: *Current Index to Journals in Education.*

77. **Education**. Vol. 1-. Chula Vista, Calif.: Project Innovation, 1880-. quarterly. $30.00 (institutions). ISSN: 0013-1172.

Concerned with all levels of education, the focus is on teaching and innovative practices. Research-based, theoretical, or essay articles are included. Its focus is generally within the U.S., although international aspects are also considered. Indexed in: *Education Index, Higher Education Abstracts, Psychological Abstracts, Sociological Abstracts.*

78. **Education Digest**. Vol. 1-. Ann Arbor, Mich.: Prakken Publications, 1935-. monthly. $45.00. ISSN: 0013-127X.

Directed to the busy educator, this digest provides condensed versions of journal articles and reports, highlighting the findings most likely to be of interest. Longer than abstracts, but still brief enough to absorb during a hectic schedule, the condensed material focuses on current issues such as school violence and school reform. Regular columns include a research report briefly summarizing recent research, news from Washington, reviews of recent publications, and association meetings being held in the coming month. Indexed in: *Education Index, Exceptional Child Education Resources.*

79. **Education Week**. Vol. 1-. Bethesda, Md.: Editorial Projects in Education, 1989-. 43 issues per year. $69.94. ISSN: 0277-4232.

For keeping informed about current issues and policies in education it is critical to have this weekly newspaper on hand. Regular features include national and state reports of activities, federal legislation, upcoming events, and job advertisements. The annual issue, *Quality Counts*, provides a report card on public education in all 50 states. Indexed in: *Education Index*.

80. **Educational Forum**. Vol. 1-. West Lafayette, Ind.: Kappa Delta Pi, 1936-. quarterly. $20.00 (nonmembers). ISSN: 0013-1725.

With a focus on educational improvement, scholarly articles that relate to practice, current issues such as school vouchers, and the teaching profession appear in this publication. Book reviews, thematic issues, and responses to published articles are regular features. Indexed in: *Education Index, Educational Administration Abstracts, Multicultural Education Abstracts*.

81. **Educational Horizons**. Vol. 1-. Bloomington, Ind.: Pi Lambda Theta, 1921-. quarterly. $18.00. ISSN: 0013-175X.

As the official publication of Pi Lambda Theta, an international honor society and professional association in education, this journal is dedicated to presenting new research, scholarly essays, and book reviews on current topics within education. Whether the topic is school violence, teacher certification, tracking, or national standards, each article is research-based, written by researchers or practitioners, and addresses current and often controversial areas. Indexed in: *Current Index to Journals in Education, Education Index, Exceptional Child Education Resources, Linguistics and Language Behavior Abstracts, Multicultural Education Abstracts, Special Educational Needs Abstracts*.

82. **Educational Leadership**. Vol. 1-. Alexandria, Va.: Association for Supervision and Curriculum Development (ASCD), 1943-. 8 issues per year. $36.00. ISSN: 0013-1784.

Association information, book reviews, and essay and opinion articles appear in this ASCD publication directed to elementary, middle school, and secondary school leaders. The topics covered include curriculum instruction, supervision, and leadership. Indexed in: *Current Index to Journals in Education, Education Index, Exceptional Child Education Resources, Multicultural Education Abstracts, Social Sciences Citation Index*.

83. **Educational Policy**. Vol. 1-. Thousand Oaks, Calif.: Corwin Press, 1987-. 6 issues per year. $275.00 (institutions). ISSN: 0895-9048.

Special thematic issues, philosophical or historical essays, action research articles, analytical papers and ethnographic studies are presented in this interdisciplinary journal. Educational policy in a variety of educational and nonschool settings is addressed at the local, national and international levels. Indexed in: *Current Index to Journals in Education, Educational Administration Abstracts, Higher Education Abstracts, Multicultural Education Abstracts, Social Sciences Citation Index, Sociology of Education Abstracts.*

84. **Educational Studies**. Vol. 1-. Abingdon, Oxfordshire, Eng.: Carfax, 1975-. 3 issues per year. $604.00 (institutions). ISSN: 0305-5698.

International in scope, and focused on research, applied, and theoretical studies in all areas of education and its related disciplines, this journal provides a forum for a very diverse selection of reports on the history and current conditions and issues in education. Also includes book reviews. Indexed in: *British Education Index, Current Index to Journals in Education, Education Index, Educational Administration Abstracts, Multicultural Education Abstracts, Psychological Abstracts, Research into Higher Education Abstracts, Social Sciences Citation Index, Sociology of Education Abstracts, Special Educational Needs Abstracts.*

85. **Gender and Education**. Vol. 1-. Abingdon, Oxfordshire, Eng.: Carfax, 1989-. quarterly. $544.00 (institutions). ISSN: 0954-0253.

Thematic issues, book reviews, and research and essay articles are included in this international journal devoted to gender and education issues. All educational levels are covered in a variety of formal and informal educational settings. Indexed in: *British Education Index, Current Index to Journals in Education, Education Index, Multicultural Education Abstracts, Sociological Abstracts.*

86. **Harvard Educational Review**. Vol. 1-. Cambridge, Mass.: Harvard Graduate School of Education, 1931-. quarterly. $79.00 (institutions). ISSN: 0017-8055.

One of the best known journals in the field of education, *HER* provides a forum for articles related to research, practice, evaluation, and theory at all levels of education. Includes book reviews. Formerly *Harvard Teachers Record*. Indexed in: *Book Review Index, Current Index to Journals in Education, Education Index, Historical Abstracts, Psychological Abstracts, Research into Higher Education, Sociology of Education Abstracts.*

87. **Initiatives**. Vol. 1-. Washington, D.C.: National Association for Women in Education, 1938-. quarterly. $75.00 (institutions). ISSN: 1042-413X.

The education, interests, needs, and personal and professional development of women and girls are addressed in the journal of NAWE. Research reports, theoretical and practical articles, essays, and book reviews appear in this quarterly publication. Indexed in: *Current Index to Journals in Education, Education Index, Higher Education Abstracts.*

88. **Instructor**. Vol. 1-. Jefferson City, Mo.: Scholastic, 1891-. 8 issues per year. $19.95. ISSN: 1049-5851.

Filled with practical suggestions for classroom activities, parent involvement, and case studies, this magazine also offers reviews of classroom materials and media, and techniques for incorporating technology in the classroom. Reproducible and pull-out units highlight the activity section. Valuable aid to the elementary and intermediate classroom teacher. Indexed in: *Current Index to Journals in Education, Education Index, Exceptional Child Education Resources.*

89. **Interchange: A Quarterly Review of Education**. Vol. 1-. Dordrecht, The Netherlands: Kluwer, 1970-. quarterly. $211.50. ISSN: 0826-4805.

Issues and trends in education, educational theory, research, policy, history, philosophy, and practices are all likely to be explored in this refereed journal. Taking a provocative stance, many articles are included with contradictory responses and further responses. All levels of education within an international context are included. Indexed in: *Canadian Education Index, Current Index to Journals in Education, Education Index, Educational Administration Abstracts, Multicultural Education Abstracts, Psychological Abstracts, Sociology of Education Abstracts.*

90. **International Review of Education**. Vol. 1-. Dordrecht, The Netherlands: Kluwer Academic, 1955-. bimonthly. $192.50 (institutions). ISSN: 0020-8566.

Edited by the UNESCO Institute for Education, this publication includes analytical articles with an international focus on policy issues, educational trends, and learning innovations. Contents are published in English, French, or German and include book reviews, case studies, commentaries, and research reports. Indexed in: *British Education Index, Current Index to Journals in Education, Education Index, Sociology of Education Abstracts.*

91. **Journal of Education**. Vol. 1-. Boston: Boston University School of Education, 1875-. 3 issues per year. $37.00 (institutions). ISSN: 0022-0574.

Each issue of this general education journal has a thematic focus. Published since 1875, the contents address contemporary education through scholarly, analytical, and reflective articles. Indexed in: *Current Index to Journals in Education, Education Index, Educational Administration Abstracts, Multicultural Education Abstracts, Psychological Abstracts, Sociology of Education Abstracts.*

92. **Journal of Education for Teaching**. Vol. 1-. Abingdon, Oxfordshire, Eng.: Carfax, 1975-. 3 issues per year. $392.00 (institutions). ISSN: 0260-7476.

Formerly *British Journal of Teacher Education*, the new title reflects the international focus on all aspects of teacher training and education. Book reviews, research reports, commentaries, and research and scholarly articles are included. Also available electronically. Indexed in: *Current Index to Journals in Education, Education Index, Higher Education Abstracts, Linguistics and Language Behavior Abstracts, Multicultural Education Abstracts, Research into Higher Education Abstracts, Social Sciences Citation Index, Sociology of Education Abstracts.*

93. **Journal of General Education**. Vol. 1-. University Park, Pa.: Pennsylvania State University Press, 1946-. quarterly-. $42.50. ISSN: 0021-3667.

Current educational issues such as school reform, teacher education, basic skills, and multicultural education are addressed in this general education forum. Addressed to all levels of education, the contents include book reviews, research articles, essays, and reports of research and practice. Indexed in: *Current Index to Journals in Education, Education Index, Exceptional Child Education Resources, Higher Education Abstracts.*

94. **Journal of Teacher Education**. Vol. 1-. Washington, D.C.: American Association of Colleges for Teacher Education (AACTE), 1950-. 5 issues per year. $125.00 (institutions). ISSN: 0022-4871.

Thematic issues, book reviews, and conceptual and empirical articles are regular features of this AACTE publication. All topics related to teacher education are considered. Indexed in: *Current Index to Journals in Education, Education Index, Educational Administration Abstracts, Multicultural Education Abstracts, Psychological Abstracts, Social Sciences Citation Index, Sociology of Education Abstracts.*

95. **Learning and Instruction: The Journal of the European Association for Research on Learning and Instruction**. Vol. 1-. Exeter, Eng.: Elsevier Science, 1991-. quarterly. $373.00 (institutions). ISSN: 0959-4752.

Issued as a companion volume to *International Journal of Educational Research*, the focus is on research on learning and instruction, particularly within the European community. The areas of learning, development, and teaching at all educational levels and settings are addressed through research articles, methodological reports, and review essays. Indexed in: *Australian Education Index, Current Index to Journals in Education, Multicultural Education Abstracts, Psychological Abstracts, Social Sciences Citation Index*.

96. **Mailbox Teacher**. Vol. 1-. Greensboro, N.C.: The Education Center, Inc., 1972-. 4 issues per year. $19.95. ISSN: 1098-5670.

Formerly titled *Learning*, this magazine offers suggestions, ideas, and activities for the busy K-6 classroom teacher. Whether the issue is coping with limited time, difficult students, or classroom safety, practical solutions are provided by teacher-practitioners. Regular features include inspirational stories, humorous anecdotes, and quick tips. Indexed in: *Current Index to Journals in Education, Education Index*.

97. **Peabody Journal of Education**. Vol. 1-. Mahwah, N.J.: Lawrence Erlbaum, 1923-. quarterly. $125.00 (institutions). ISSN: 0161-956X.

Each issue of this research journal has a thematic focus on issues of relevance to the field of education. Drawing its editorial board (and name) from the Peabody College of Vanderbilt University, this publication has a long and well-established history as a forum for research in policy issues and trends in education. Indexed in: *Current Index to Journals in Education, Education Index, Exceptional Child Education Resources, Linguistics and Language Behavior Abstracts, Research into Higher Education Abstracts, Social Sciences Citation Index, Sociological Abstracts*.

98. **Phi Delta Kappan**. Vol. 1-. Bloomington, Ind.: Phil Delta Kappa International, 1915-. 10 issues per year. $46.00 (institutions). ISSN: 0031-7217.

One of the leading journals in education that keeps track of issues, trends, and policies, *Phi Delta Kappan* publishes articles related to educational research, leadership, and service. Regular features include legal cases, federal activity, and editorial commentaries. Also available electronically. Indexed in: *Current Index to Journals in Education, Education Index*.

99. **Research Papers in Education: Policy and Practice**. Vol. 1-. London: Routledge, 1986-. 3 issues per year. $260.00 (institutions). ISSN: 0267-1522.

Internationally-focused journal on education across the life span offers lengthy research articles dealing with educational policy and practice. Book reviews are also included. Indexed in: *Current Index to Journals in Education, Multicultural Education Abstracts, Sociology of Education Abstracts, Special Educational Needs Abstracts*.

100. **Review of Education/Pedagogy/Cultural Studies**. Vol. 1-. Newark, N.J.: IPD, 1975-. quarterly. $79.00. ISSN: 1071-4413.

Lengthy essays about books and the field of education and pedagogy are the hallmark of this publication. Contributions are from a variety of disciplines. Indexed in: *Current Index to Journals in Education, Education Index, Educational Administration Abstracts, Multicultural Education Abstracts*.

101. **Rural Educator**. Vol. 1-. Fort Collins, Colo.: National Rural Education Association, 1980-. 3 issues per year. $30.00. ISSN: 0273-446X.

Rural Educator focuses on rural education and rural development, with a strong emphasis on promoting interaction between university faculty and rural educators. Ideas, resources, and activities for rural teachers are included as part of the incorporated magazine, *Country Teacher*. Indexed in: *Current Index to Journals in Education, Education Index, Multicultural Education Abstracts*.

102. **School Community Journal**. Vol. 1-. Lincoln, Ill.: Center for the School Community, 1991-. 2 issues per year. $35.00 (institutions). ISSN: 1059-308X.

This journal focuses on the school as a community, rather than the interactions between the external community and the school. Research articles, essays, reports, and program descriptions about the school as an entity whose members have shared values are presented. Indexed in: *Current Index to Journals in Education*.

103. **Sociology of Education**. Vol. 1-. Washington, D.C.: American Sociological Association, 1927-. quarterly. $95.00 (institutions). ISSN: 0038-0407.

Focusing on the study of sociology of education and social development, the articles in this journal examine how individuals, institutions, and the educational process affect each other. Of interest to educators, sociologists, and those concerned with educational policy. Indexed in: *Current Index to Journals in Education, Education*

Index, Educational Administration Abstracts, Higher Education Abstracts, Multicultural Education Abstracts, Psychological Abstracts, Social Sciences Citation Index, Sociology of Education Abstracts.

104.   **Teacher Educator**. Vol. 1-. Muncie, Ind.: Teachers College, Ball State University, 1965-. quarterly. $25.00 (institutions). ISSN: 0887-8730.

Research articles on teacher education are the focus of this journal, which is also the official journal of the Indiana Association of Teacher Educators. All aspects of teacher education are considered including content area preparation, teacher as learner, and classroom management. Also available electronically. Indexed in: *Current Index to Journals in Education, Education Index.*

105.   **Teachers College Record**. Vol. 1-. New York: Teachers College, Columbia University, 1900-. quarterly. $70.00 (institutions). ISSN: 0161-4681.

Published since 1900, this is a highly regarded journal that offers a forum for commentary, analysis, and research in all areas of education. Book and essay reviews are regular features. Indexed in: *Current Index to Journals in Education, Education Index, Educational Administration Abstracts, Multicultural Education Abstracts, Psychological Abstracts, Social Sciences Citation Index, Sociology of Education Abstracts.*

106.   **Teaching and Teacher Education**. Vol. 1-. Exeter, Eng.: Elsevier Science, 1985-. 8 issues per year. $641.00 (institutions). ISSN: 0742-051X.

Theoretical and conceptual analyses, research reviews, and scholarly articles focusing on teachers, teaching, and teacher education at any level are contained in this international journal. Research that informs practice is emphasized. Also available electronically. Indexed in: *Current Index to Journals in Education, Education Index, Psychological Abstracts, Social Sciences Citation Index, Sociology of Education Abstracts.*

107.   **Teaching Education**. http://www.teachingeducation.com. Vol. 1-. Columbia, S.C.: College of Education, University of South Carolina, 1987-. 2 issues per year. $35.00 (institutions). ISSN: 1047-6210.

Published by the University of South Carolina in collaboration with Wright State University, this semiannual journal provides descriptions of undergraduate and graduate education courses,

scholarly essays, book and media reviews, and collaborative classroom practices. Published electronically with supplemental material. Indexed in: *Current Index to Journals in Education, Education
Index, Sociology of Education Abstracts.*

108. **Teaching Pre K-8**. Vol. 1-. Norwalk, Conn.: Early Years, Inc.,
1971-. 8 issues per year. $23.97. ISSN: 0891-4508.

Formerly *Early Years*, this teacher resource offers practical
classroom strategies and activities, teaching tips, reviews of children's books and teaching tools, and updates on education issues
and news. Valuable journal for the busy elementary and middle
school teacher. Indexed in: *Current Index to Journals in Education,
Education Index, Exceptional Child Education Resources.*

109. **Theory into Practice**. Vol. 1-. Columbus, Ohio: College of Education, Ohio State University, 1962-. quarterly. $68.00 (institutions).
ISSN: 0040-5841.

Each issue of this publication has a thematic focus, incorporating diverse views on a single topic. Supported by research, each
article contributes to a discussion of an educational issue, policy,
or theory. Indexed in: *Current Index to Journals in Education,
Education Index, Educational Administration Abstracts, Multicultural Education Abstracts, Psychological Abstracts, Sociology of
Education Abstracts.*

110. **Urban Education**. Vol. 1-. Thousand Oaks, Calif.: Corwin Press,
1966-. 5 issues per year. $275.00 (institutions). ISSN: 0042-0859.

Keeping abreast of issues in urban education is the focus of
this journal. Articles about multiculturalism, parental involvement,
community support, low-income students, and drop-out prevention
are typical of the contents. Book reviews and annual thematic issues
are also featured. Indexed in: *Current Index to Journals in Education, Education Index, Educational Administration Abstracts, Multicultural Education Abstracts, Social Sciences Citation Index,
Sociology of Education Abstracts.*

Biographies

111. Aldrich, Richard, and Gordon, Peter. **Dictionary of British Educationists**. London: Woburn Press, 1989. 272 p. $35.00. LC: 88-
12114. ISBN: 0-7130-0177-1.

Four hundred and fifty educators from 1800 on are included
in this biographical dictionary. Criteria for inclusion are that each
individual must be deceased and British (or have had a major impact

on British education). Arranged in alphabetical sequence, most entries include a selective bibliography and a list of the educator's publications. Portraits of some subjects enliven the text, as do reproductions of title pages of significant works. To aid the researcher of British educators, the authors have included a brief list of additional sources and repositories of biographical information.

112. Gordon, Peter, and Aldrich, Richard. **Biographical Dictionary of North American and European Educationists**. London: Woburn Press, 1997. 528 p. $49.50. LC: 96-37182. ISBN: 0-7130-0205-0.

Produced as a companion volume to *Dictionary of British Educationists*, this volume offers brief biographies of European and North American figures in the field of education. Included are educators whose careers occurred after 1800, and who are now deceased. From Mary McLeod Bethune to Maria Montessori and beyond, each entry provides a brief personal history followed by significant contributions to education. Sources of additional biographical information are appended at the end of the book.

113. Ohles, Frederik, Ohles, Shirley M., and Ramsay, John G. **Biographical Dictionary of Modern American Educators**. Westport, Conn.: Greenwood, 1997. 432 p. $79.50. LC: 97-6413. ISBN: 0-313-29133-0.

Limited to educators who made a significant impact on the field, and who were born before 1935 or who are deceased, this dictionary provides brief biographical sketches of 410 individuals. Ranging from the well known such as John Goodlad, to the more obscure, the entries highlight the unique contributions of each person. Appendixes provide access by place of birth, states of major service, field of work (e.g., measurement and evaluation), chronology of birth years, and important dates in American education. Useful source for biographical information.

114. Ohles, John F., ed. **Biographical Dictionary of American Educators**. Westport, Conn.: Greenwood Press, 1978. 3 vol. $195.00. LC: 77-84750. ISBN: 0-8371-9893-3.

Biographical sketches of 1,665 major figures in the field of education are included in this three volume set. Eminent educators who had reached the age of 60, retired, or were deceased prior to 1975 are included. The inclusion of women and individuals from different populations enhances this somewhat dated source. Sketches include basic personal information, a description of the individual's contributions to education, and references to further information. Appendixes include place of birth, state of major service, field of specialization, a chronology of birth years, and important dates relating to American education. An extensive index greatly enhances this source. Updated in part in *Biographical Dictionary of Modern American Educators.*

115. **Who's Who in American Education 1996-1997**. 5th ed. New Providence, N.J.: Marquis Who's Who, 1995. 1,092 p. $159.95. LC: 89-649424. ISBN: 0-8379-2704-8.

Over 23,000 sketches of educators at the elementary, secondary, and higher levels of education are included in this directory. Each sketch includes standard personal and professional information as well as significant achievements, publications, and awards. Indexes by professional activity or specialization, and by recent awards received are included. Useful source of biographical information about contemporary educators.

2

EDUCATIONAL TECHNOLOGY
AND MEDIA

Dictionaries and Encyclopedias

116.   Ellington, Henry, and Harris, Duncan. **Dictionary of Instructional Technology**. London: Kogan Page, 1986. 189 p. $37.50. LC: 82-28530. ISBN: 0-89397-243-6.

Supported by the Association for Educational and Training Technology (AETT), this dictionary provides brief definitions of British and U.S. terms used in instructional technology. Due to the rapid changes in technology, many newer relevant terms are not included, indeed, were not even conceived of, when this was published. However, many of the standard terms remain the same, and historical terms such as "lantern slide" remind educators just how many technological advances have been made. Also includes many terms for assessment techniques and types of testing tools.

Directories and Almanacs

117.   **The Latest and Best of TESS: The Educational Software Selector**. Hampton Bays, N.Y.: Educational Products Information Exchange (EPIE), 1993. 217 p. $19.95. ISBN: 0-916087-16-6.

The 1993 edition of this directory includes Macintosh and IBM compatible software. Included are 1,350 programs considered to be the most recent or the best of currently available software. Organized by subject, each entry includes the product title, hardware requirements, grade levels, type, components, a description, and source information. When available, citations to published reviews are provided. In addition to classroom materials, record keeping software useful to administrators and teachers and other related administrative activities are also included. A directory of software suppliers, a glossary, and an index by product name are appended.

118.   **Only the Best: The Annual Guide to the Highest-Rated Educational Software and Multimedia**. Alexandria, Va.: Association for Supervision and Curriculum Development, 1997. 129 p. $29.00 (nonmembers); $25.00 (members). ISSN: 1053-4326.

This guide to stringently evaluated software and multimedia offers descriptions, technical requirements, costs, evaluations, and sources of reviews for each entry. Subject and title indexes make locating appropriate K-12 software simple. Produced by a reputable organization with carefully selected evaluators, this guide lives up to its title.

Guides, Handbooks, and Yearbooks

119.   Berger, James L., ed. **Educators Guide to Free Videotapes**. 45th ed. Randolph, Wis.: Educators Progress Service, 1998. 338 p. $27.95. LC: 55-2784. ISBN: 0-87708-307-X.

An annual publication from Educators Progress Service that provides information about free videotapes for use by teachers. Videotapes are listed by topic, with indexes providing access by title, subject, and source. Introductory matter includes a sample request letter and form for evaluating materials.

120.   Branch, Robert Maribe, and Fitzgerald, Mary Ann, ed. **Educational Media and Technology Yearbook**. 23rd ed. Englewood, Colo.: Libraries Unlimited, 1998. 296 p. $65.00. ISSN: 8755-2094. ISBN: 1-56308-591-7. Published in cooperation with the ERIC Clearinghouse on Information and Technology and the Association for Educational Communications and Technology.

Published since 1973, the *Yearbook* combines an annual review of technology trends in education with a directory of graduate programs in instructional technology, a bibliography of print and nonprint sources, and a list of relevant organizations and associations. The essays by practitioners and researchers address the current state of educational technology, while the various directories provide valuable sources for further information. Indexed in: *Current Index to Journals in Education*.

121. **Educators Guide to Free Films, Filmstrips and Slides**. 58th ed. Randolph, Wis.: Educators Progress Service, 1998. 221 p. $36.95. LC: 50-11650.

Several categories of K-12 free media materials are listed in this guide. Ranging from accident prevention to social problems, materials offer an array of free supplementary classroom materials. As always, the publisher includes a sample letter for requesting free materials or booking items for loan. Subject, title, and source indexes enhance the usefulness of this guide.

122. Jonassen, David H., ed. **Handbook of Research for Educational Communications and Technology**. New York: Simon & Schuster Macmillan, 1996. 1,267 p. $85.00. LC: 96-21386. ISBN: 0-02-864663-0.

Developed as a project of the Association for Educational Communications and Technology (AECT), this handbook provides a voluminous overview of the history, current issues and challenges, and future of educational technology and communications. Five sections offer 42 chapters on the foundations for research; hard technologies: media-related research; soft technologies: instructional and informational design research; instructional strategies research: issues of organization and change; and research methodologies. Each chapter includes extensive references, and a comprehensive index is provided.

123. Nehmer, Kathleen Suttles, ed. **Guide to Free Computer Materials**. 16th ed. Randolph, Wis.: Educators Progress Service, 1998. 335 p. $38.95.

This guide to free computer resources lists materials under various subject headings as well as systems and hardware resources, and software, including shareware. Full ordering information is included for each item. In some instances, brochures and videotapes are available on these topics; in others, the actual software is provided. In addition to title, source, and subject indexes, a glossary of computer terminology is included.

124. Rider, Betty L., ed. **Diversity in Technology Education**. New York: McGraw-Hill, 1998. 198 p. (*Council on Technology Teacher Education Yearbook* v. 47). ISBN: 0-02-831274-0; 0-02-831274-0 (CD-ROM version).

The 47th yearbook of the Council on Technology Teacher Education has a focus on diversity in technology education. An historical overview of the presence (or lack) of underrepresented groups in technology education is followed by the current status of underrepresented groups in this field, and changing conditions and ways in which to improve the situation. The 47th yearbook is also available as a CD-ROM, which accompanies the print version. Each of the yearbooks has a special thematic focus. Recent yearbooks have addressed elementary school technology, technology and the quality of life, foundations of technology education, and other very specialized topics.

125.   Robin, Bernard, Price, Jerry D., Willis, Jerry, and Willis, Dee Anna, ed. **Technology and Teacher Education Annual, 1996**. Charlottesville, Va.: Association for the Advancement of Computing in Education (AACE), 1996. 1,063 p. $45.00. ISBN: 1-880094-20-7. "Proceedings of SITE 96—Seventh International Conference of the Society for Information Technology and Teacher Education (SITE), Phoenix, Arizona; March 13-19, 1996."

The AACE division, Society for Information Technology and Teacher Education, issues an annual publication that addresses the use of information technology in teacher education, including theoretical research and professional practice. Each annual publication has a thematic focus that reflects the annual conference topic. The papers included in each volume present a valuable "state of the art" briefing in teacher education and technology.

Journals

126.   **British Journal of Educational Technology**. Vol. 1-. Oxford, Eng.: Blackwell, 1970-. quarterly. $216.00. ISSN: 0007-1013.

Sponsored by the British Educational Communications and Technology Agency, this journal focuses on educational training and information technology. Articles that address theory, applications, and development of educational technology and communications are featured. Book reviews and brief reports supplement the longer articles included in each issue. Indexed in: *British Education Index, Current Index to Journals in Education, Education Index, Educational Administration Abstracts, Social Sciences Citation Index.*

127.   **Educational Technology Research and Development**. Vol. 1-. Washington, D.C.: Association for Educational Communications and Technology (AECT), 1953-. quarterly. $65.00. ISSN: 1042-1629. Former titles *AV Communication Review; Educational Communication and Technology; Journal of Instructional Development.*

Book reviews, research reports and articles, development and practice reports, and special thematic issues related to educational technology are regular features of this journal. Valuable resource for practitioners, educators and administrators concerned with educational technology. Indexed in: *Current Index to Journals in Education, Education Index, Psychological Abstracts, Social Sciences Citation Index.*

128. **Educational Technology: The Magazine for Managers of Change in Education**. Vol. 1-. Englewood Cliffs, N.J.: Educational Technology Publications, 1961-. bimonthly. $119.00. ISSN: 0013-1962.

Educational technology/learning environments and Web-based courses are just some of the topics addressed in this magazine. Descriptive, essay, and research articles are directed to educators and administrators concerned with technology at all educational levels. Indexed in: *Current Index to Journals in Education, Education Index, Educational Administration Abstracts, Exceptional Child Education Resources, Psychological Abstracts, Social Sciences Citation Index.*

129. **Journal of Computers in Mathematics and Science Teaching**. Vol.1-. Charlottesville, Va.: Association for the Advancement of Computing in Education, 1981-. quarterly. $93.00 (institutions). ISSN: 0731-9258.

This specialized journal focuses on the use of electronic and computer technologies in mathematics and science teaching in a variety of educational settings. Articles encompass research, theory, philosophy, and practice. Indexed in: *Current Index to Journals in Education.*

130. **Journal of Research on Computing in Education**. Vol. 1-. Eugene, Ore.: International Society for Technology in Education (ISTE), 1967-. quarterly. $78.00 (nonmembers). ISSN: 0888-6504.

All levels of education are addressed in this ISTE publication with its focus on project or system descriptions; literature reviews; and theoretical, conceptual, or research articles. Student learning, teacher use of technologies, and computer literacy are a few of the topics addressed. Indexed in: *Current Index to Journals in Education, Education Index, Educational Administration Abstracts.*

131. **Journal of Technology Education**. http://scholar.lib.vt.edu/ejournals/ JTE/jte.html. Vol. 1-. Blacksburg, Va.: Virginia Polytechnic Institute, 1989-. 2 issues per year. $20.00 (institutions). ISSN: 1045-1064.

    Although available in print, this technology journal is also appropriately available via the World Wide Web. Issued twice annually, the refereed articles focus on technology research, philosophy, and theory. Also included are book reviews, essays, and commentaries. Indexed in: *Current Index to Journals in Education.*

132. **T.H.E. Journal**. Vol. 1-. Tustin, Calif.: T.H.E. Journal, 1973-. 11 issues per year. $29.00 (free to qualified educators on a limited basis). ISSN: 0192-592X.

    T.H.E. Journal (Technological Horizons in Education) provides a source of information on technological innovations and practices useful to educators and administrators. Topics such as technology and distance education, collaborative learning, and digital applications as they impact the educational process and delivery of education are included. Indexed in: *Current Index to Journals in Education, Education Index, Educational Administration Abstracts.*

133. **Technology and Learning**. Vol. 1-. San Francisco: Miller Freeman, Inc., 1980-. 10 issues per year. $29.95. ISSN: 1053-6728.

    Essays, classroom activities, articles on practice, teaching tips, and product reviews are featured in this journal devoted to incorporating technology into the learning process. Directed to elementary and secondary level educators. Indexed in: *Current Index to Journals in Education, Education Index.*

134. **Technology Teacher**. Vol. 1-. Reston, Va.: International Technology Education Association, 1939-. 8 issues per year. $70.00 (institutions). ISSN: 0746-3537.

    Technology Teacher, formerly *Man/Society/Technology*, has as its purpose the development and improvement of technology education at the national and international levels. The journal includes association news, learning activities, classroom resources, essays, commentaries, and research and practice articles. Indexed in: *Current Index to Journals in Education, Education Index.*

135. **TechTrends: For Leaders in Education and Training**. Vol. 1-. Washington, D.C.: Association for Educational Communications and Technology (AECT), 1956-. 6 issues per year. $40.00 (non-members). ISSN: 8756-3894.

Formerly *Instructional Innovator*, this is the official AECT journal. As such, it provides association news, reports on technological innovations in education, regular columns, new product information, and more for all levels of education. Indexed in: *Current Index to Journals in Education, Education Index, Linguistics and Language Behavior Abstracts.*

3

EARLY CHILDHOOD, ELEMENTARY, AND SECONDARY EDUCATION

Dictionaries and Encyclopedias

136. Williams, Leslie R., and Fromberg, Doris Pronin, ed. **Encyclopedia of Early Childhood Education**. New York: Garland, 1992. 518 p. (*Garland Reference Library of the Social Sciences* v. 504). $95.00. LC: 92-4579. ISBN: 0-8240-4626-9.

The index is a critical key to the contents of this work, which is arranged in six broad categories rather than alphabetically. After a brief introduction, the following five chapters address the historical and philosophical roots of early childhood practice; sociocultural, political, and economic contexts of child care and early education; perspectives on children; early childhood curricula and programs; and perspectives on educators. To find the individually-authored entries to Head Start or certified teachers, referral to the index is crucial. Most, but not all, entries include references.

Directories and Almanacs

137. Frazier, Gloria G., and Sickles, Robert N. **Directory of Innovations in High Schools**. Princeton, N.J.: Eye on Education, 1993. 400 p. $39.95. LC: 93-70824. ISBN: 1-883001-00-5.

Describing 153 innovative programs and practices in use at high schools within the U.S., this directory offers teachers, parents, and administrators a list of contacts for assistance in developing similar programs. In addition to indicating the goals for each program and the way it works and is funded, issues of concern are briefly listed as are results. The programs are presented in broad categories such as organizational innovations, changing expectations, and developing community and family support. Indexes by state, program title, and name of contact person are provided. A brief general index provides access by subject and type of program.

138. **The Handbook of Private Schools: An Annual Descriptive Survey of Independent Education**. 78th ed. Boston: Porter Sargent Publishers, 1997. 1,368 p. (*Sargent handbook series*) $90.00. ISSN: 0072-9884. ISBN: 0-87558-137-4.

   With 1,632 schools listed in the directory, this handbook provides a solid overview of private schools in the United States that offer special services or curricula for day or boarding students. A geographical listing is provided with brief descriptions of each school, its focus, costs, and enrollment. This is supplemented by a separate section of self-selected schools with full descriptions and promotional information. Brief listings of schools offering military programs, special needs programs, elementary boarding opportunities, special language instruction, or single-sex education are also provided.

139. **Patterson's American Education 1997**. 93rd ed. Mount Prospect, Ill.: Educational Directories, Inc., 1997. 850 p. $81.00. LC: 04-012953. ISSN: 0079-0230. ISBN: 0-910536-67-8.

   Now in its 93rd year of publication, this well-established directory provides information about school districts and secondary schools throughout the United States in a geographic arrangement by state and city. The 1997 edition lists 11,900 public school districts, 28,000 public secondary schools, 4,300 private and Catholic secondary schools, and over 6,000 postsecondary schools. It does not include non-graded, special education schools or nontraditional secondary schools. Together with its companion volume, *Patterson's Elementary Education*, this work provides comprehensive information in a straightforward format.

140. **Patterson's Elementary Education 1997**. 9th ed. Mount Prospect, Ill.: Educational Directories, Inc., 1997. 888 p. $81.00. LC: 89-646629. ISSN: 1044-1417. ISBN: 0-910536-68-6.

   The 1997 edition of this comprehensive work includes listings for 13,000 public school districts, 63,000 public elementary schools, and 13,000 private and Catholic elementary schools. Using the same format as the companion volume, *Patterson's American*

Education, information about each school is easily located through a geographical listing by state and city. Basic information includes school or district name, address, telephone and FAX numbers, principal or superintendent, and enrollment and grade range information. Listings for each state also include information about the state department or board of education. Excluded from this directory are non-graded, special education schools, preschools and other nontraditional elementary schools.

141. **Peterson's Private Secondary Schools, 1997-98**. 18th ed. Princeton, N.J.: Peterson's, 1997. 1,402 p. $29.95. ISSN: 1066-5366. ISBN: 1-56079-7020-9.

    Containing 1,500 listings of private or alternative schools in the United States and Canada, this directory offers background information for each institution as well as promotional information provided by self-selected schools. In addition to college preparatory schools, special needs schools are included, which serve students with a variety of special learning or social needs, and junior boarding schools for middle school students. Specialized directories also identify coeducational day schools, single-sex day schools, boarding schools, military schools, schools with a religious affiliation, and several other categories of educational opportunities. A "quick-reference chart" permits rapid identification of schools by geographical location, curricula, and type of students served.

142. **Private Independent Schools 1998**. 51st ed. Wallingford, Conn.: Bunting and Lyon, 1998. 580 p. $100.00. LC: 72-122324. ISSN: 0079-5399. ISBN: 0-913094-51-X.

    Also known as the *Bunting and Lyon Blue Book*, this directory offers multiple access points to descriptions of private independent schools. In addition to an alphabetical index to schools by name, three other indexes are provided in grid form. A geographic listing of schools in each state indicates whether the school is a day or boarding school, religious affiliation, summer programs, educational level, military programs, and so on. A special notation indicates if students with learning differences are served. An index of schools having programs for students with learning differences is also provided on a state-by-state basis. A third index indicates which schools offer summer programs. The majority of this extensive directory provides descriptions of each school, sometimes with photographs. Contact information includes e-mail, FAX number, and Web site addresses with descriptions and costs for each school. Excellent source of information about private independent schools.

143.   Rich, Elizabeth H., ed. **National Guide to Funding for Elementary and Secondary Education**. 4th ed. New York: Foundation Center, 1997. 725 p. $140.00. ISBN: 0-87954-715-4.

Includes information on more than 2,000 foundations, public charities, and corporate giving programs. Support is directed to bilingual and vocational education, nursery schools, special education, programs for gifted or minority students, testing, drop-out prevention, and many other programs in elementary or secondary education. The *Guide* provides a glossary of relevant terminology; a bibliography of funding information; a descriptive directory of funding agencies; and six indexes that cover donors, geographic access, types of support, subject access to grants and grantmakers, and an alphabetical list of grantmakers. A thorough and authoritative resource on grant funding for the elementary and secondary education sector.

Guides, Handbooks, and Yearbooks

144.   **Comparative Guide to American Elementary & Secondary Schools**. Milpitas, Calif.: Toucan Valley Publications, 1998. 774 p. $85.00. ISBN: 1-884925-61-8.

Data was drawn from the National Center for Education Statistics and reflects the 1995-1996 school year. Although schools are not ranked, a popular question from parents, it is possible to compare school districts serving 2,500 or more students using this resource. Under each state, qualifying districts are arranged by county and city. In addition to address, telephone number, grade levels, number and type of schools, enrollment, number of teachers, student/teacher ratio, expenditures per student, number of librarians and ratio to students, and number of guidance counselors and ratio to students, the ethnicity and socioeconomic status of students are also indicated. A separate city index provides access to school districts by city name when the county is not known. Fills a gap in the literature by providing comparative data in a simple, accessible form.

145.   Nehmer, Kathleen Suttles, ed. **Elementary Teachers Guide to Free Curriculum Materials 1998-1999**. 55th ed. Randolph, Wis.: Educators Progress Service, 1998. 304 p. $26.95. LC: 44-52255. ISBN: 0-87708-309-6.

Excellent source of free materials for the elementary classroom. Listings are arranged by general subject area with a brief description, grade level, and source information. Separate indexes provide access by title, subject, and source. Another index lists items new to this edition. A brief introduction explains the value and necessity for supplementary classroom materials, while an evaluation form is included for assessing such materials. Teachers are encouraged to provide feedback to the producers of classroom materials about their value and usefulness.

146. Shokraii, Nina H., and Youssef, Sarah E. **School Choice Programs: What's Happening in the States**. Washington, D.C.: Heritage Foundation, 1998. 159 p. $10.00. http://www.heritage.org/heritage/schools/.

State-by-state summaries on the status of school choice are provided in this frankly pro school choice publication. An introduction provides a current status report on school choice efforts nationally, while each state summary provides a brief profile of the state's education spending, graduation rates, and number of charter schools. Background information, developments during the previous year, position of the governor, and state contacts also appear in each state summary. A glossary of school choice terminology is very helpful. Updates between annual print publications appear on the World Wide Web.

147. Spodek, Bernard, ed. **Handbook of Research on the Education of Young Children**. New York: Macmillan, 1993. 568 p. $75.00. LC: 92-21051. ISBN: 0-02-897405-0.

Divided into four parts addressing child development and early education; foundations of early childhood educational curriculum; foundations of early childhood educational policy; and, research strategies for early childhood education, this handbook provides an overview of the history and current status of early childhood educational issues. Directed to scholars, practitioners, and policymakers, the contents are research-based articles that address different aspects of child development, education, and needs. Topics include motor development, content area education for young children, multicultural education, assessment, special populations, international comparisons in kindergarten, and future trends. Each article includes extensive references. Name and subject indexes enhance access to article contents. Valuable source of information in early childhood education.

148. Tryneski, John, ed. **Requirements for Certification of Teachers, Counselors, Librarians, Administrators for Elementary and Secondary Schools, 1998-99**. 63rd ed. Chicago: University of Chicago Press, 1998. 237 p. $38.00. LC: A43-1905. ISSN: 1047-7071. ISBN: 0-226-81318-5.

Now in its 63rd edition, this work provides current checklists of requirements for teaching in each state. Requirements for counselors, librarians, and administrators are also provided and recommendations of regional and national associations are included. Of particular use is the list of addresses for state offices of certification in the appendix.

149. Woodill, Gary A., Bernhard, Judith, and Prochner, Lawrence, ed. **International Handbook of Early Childhood Education**. New York: Garland, 1992. 562 p. (*Garland Reference Library of Social Science* v. 598). $40.00. LC: 92-23846. ISBN: 0-8240-4939-X.

Authors from forty-five countries are represented in this comparative handbook on early childhood education. Articles address the organization and curricula of early childhood education on six continents. The introductory essays on historical perspectives and a cross-national analysis are followed by reviews of individual countries. In addition to references at the end of each essay, a bibliography of English-language resources is appended as are biographies of the contributors and a subject index. Provides a useful overview of early childhood education in many countries with some cross-national comparison.

Statistical Sources

150. Fisher, Millard T., ed. **NCEA/Ganley's Catholic Schools in America**. 25th ed. Silverthorne, Colo.: Fisher Publishing Co., in cooperation with the National Catholic Education Association, 1997. [58], 207 p. $40.00.

Rather than being only a directory of Catholic schools, this is also a compendium of statistical data that provides an overview of Catholic education in the United States and Puerto Rico. Demographic data and trends in public and private education are provided as a context. This is followed by the current number of Catholic schools, their regional distribution, type, location, enrollment by various categories, and staffing. Also addressed are extended care services, Title I services, and single-sex schools. A computer listing of schools with addresses, telephone, grades, enrollment and the name of the principal comprises the bulk of this specialized directory.

Journals

151. **Childhood Education: Infancy Through Early Adolescence**. Vol. 1-. Olney, Md.: Association for Childhood Education International, 1924-. 6 issues per year. $55.00 (institutions). ISSN: 0009-4056.

Written for educators working with children from birth to age 13, the journal supports a child-centered approach to education that incorporates the influence of school, home, and the community. Classroom activities, research articles, reviews of children's and professional books, and association information are included in each issue. In addition to quarterly issues, the subscription includes an annual thematic issue and an issue with an international focus. Also available electronically. Indexed in: *Child Development Abstracts, Current Index to Journals in Education, Education Index, Psychological Abstracts.*

152. **Clearing House**. Vol. 1-. Washington, D.C.: Heldref, 1920-. bimonthly. $64.00 (institutions). ISSN: 0009-8655.

Of interest to middle school and high school teachers and administrators, this journal offers research articles, practical reports, and opinion essays in all areas of education. Valuable resource for educators. Indexed in: *Business Education Index, Current Index to Journals in Education, Education Index, Educational Administration Abstracts.*

153. **Dimensions of Early Childhood**. Vol. 1-. Little Rock, Ark.: Southern Early Childhood Association, 1973-. quarterly. ISSN: 1068-6177.

Directed to early childhood educators, early childhood program administrators, and others concerned with early childhood issues, the journal of the Southern Early Childhood Association provides practical information and research-based articles. Association information and book reviews are also included. Indexed in: *Current Index to Journals in Education.*

154. **Early Childhood Education Journal**. Vol. 1-. New York: Human Sciences Press, 1973-. quarterly. $195.00. ISSN: 1082-3301.

Directed to early childhood educators, child care providers, researchers, and early childhood program administrators, the contents of this journal include refereed articles, case studies, program descriptions, and print and nonprint media reviews. Former title *Day Care and Early Education.* Indexed in: *Current Index to*

Journals in Education, Education Index, Exceptional Child Education Resources, Sociological Abstracts.

155. **Early Childhood Research Quarterly**. http://www.udel.edu/ecrq. Vol. 1-. Stamford, Conn.: Ablex, 1986-. quarterly. $195.00 (institutions). ISSN: 0885-2006.

   Sponsored by the National Association for the Education of Young Children, this journal presents research-based articles on all topics related to the care and education of young children. Book reviews are also included in this scholarly publication. Indexed in: *Current Index to Journals in Education.*

156. **Early Education and Development**. Vol. 1-. Wilmington, Del.: Wide Range, Inc., 1989-. quarterly. $145.00. ISSN: 1040-9289.

   Research-based articles with implications for practice and general policy articles are the focus of this journal. Early childhood educators, child care providers, researchers, and special education providers will find material of value. Indexed in: *Child Development Abstracts, Current Index to Journals in Education, Education Index, Psychological Abstracts.*

157. **Elementary School Journal**. Vol. 1-. Chicago: University of Chicago Press, 1900-. 5 issues per year. $86.00 (institutions). ISSN: 0013-5984.

   With a focus on educational theory and research and its impact on teaching within the elementary and middle school classroom, this is one of the key journals within elementary education. Indexed in: *Current Index to Journals in Education, Education Index, Educational Administration Abstracts, Linguistics and Language Behavior Abstracts, Psychological Abstracts, Sociology of Education Abstracts.*

158. **High School Journal**. Vol. 1-. Chapel Hill, N.C.: School of Education, University of North Carolina, 1917-. 4 issues per year. $28.00 (institutions). ISSN: 0018-1498.

   Special thematic issues, research and essay articles, and reports of practice are included in this journal focused on secondary education. Indexed in: *Current Index to Journals in Education, Education Index.*

159. **Independent School**. Vol. 1-. Washington, D.C.: National Association of Independent Schools, 1941-. 3 issues per year. $17.50 (nonmembers). ISSN: 0145-9635.

Directed to those with interests in independent schools, particularly administrators, the contents of this journal tend to be essays, brief reports, and association news. Includes classified advertising aimed at private schools, and job openings.

160. **Journal of Research in Childhood Education: An International Journal of Research on the Education of Children, Infancy Through Early Adolescence**. Vol. 1-. Wheaton, Md.: Association for Childhood Education International (ACEI), 1986-. 2 issues per year. $38.00. ISSN: 0256-8543.

With its emphasis on childhood education through early adolescence, this journal includes a mixture of empirical and theoretical articles, case studies, observation studies, ethnographic and cross-cultural studies, and international research reports. Indexed in: *Current Index to Journals in Education, Education Index, Multicultural Education Abstracts, Psychological Abstracts, Social Sciences Citation Index, Sociology of Education Abstracts*.

161. **Middle School Journal**. Vol. 1-. Columbus, Ohio: National Middle School Association, 1970-. 5 issues per year. $35.00. ISSN: 0094-0771.

Filled with publication and conference announcements and news from the National Middle School Association, this journal also presents articles dealing with effective practice and teaching at the middle school level. Other topics routinely addressed are technology in the classroom and research into practice. Indexed in: *Education Index*.

162. **Young Children**. Vol. 1-. Washington, D.C.: National Association for the Education of Young Children (NAEYC), 1944-. 6 issues per year. $30.00 (nonmembers). ISSN: 0044-0728.

NAEYC's official journal includes association news, research-based articles with implications for practice, updates on federal legislation, and book reviews. Articles focus on methods for working with young children, needs of young children, and interacting effectively with parents. Indexed in: *Current Index to Journals in Education, Education Index, Exceptional Child Education Resources, Linguistics and Language Behavior Abstracts, Psychological Abstracts, Social Sciences Citation Index*.

Biographies

163.   Peltzman, Barbara Ruth. **Pioneers of Early Childhood Education: A Bio-Bibliographical Guide**. Westport, Conn.: Greenwood Press, 1998. 140 p. $65.00. LC: 97-26907. ISBN: 0-313-30404-1.

Brief biographical information about selected leaders in early childhood education, who are now deceased, is presented in this work. However, bibliographical sources of information about the individual's work and its impact on early childhood education are the strength of this guide. Following a brief biographical summary of each person's educational contribution, primary and secondary sources of information for further study are listed. Each source includes a full citation and a brief summary of the contents. In addition to the expected inclusion of such leaders as Froebel and Montessori, lesser known figures who were involved in the advancement of early childhood education for underrepresented populations are also profiled. A chronological list of pre-modern and modern pioneers is appended, as is a brief bibliography and a slim index. Useful source of information for a specialized area.

4

HIGHER EDUCATION

Bibliographies

164. Sparks, Linda. **Institutions of Higher Education: An International Bibliography**. Westport, Conn.: Greenwood Press, 1990. 478 p. (*Bibliographies and Indexes in Education* v. 9). $85.00. LC: 89-29355. ISSN: 0742-6917. ISBN: 0-313-26686-7.

   Histories of institutions of higher education are presented in this international bibliography. References are to books, reports, dissertations, and theses that chronicle the history of community colleges, universities, seminaries, colleges, and specialized postsecondary institutions. Arranged alphabetically by country and state, each institution is listed within its geographic region. All names of institutions are written in English, but the references are in the language in which they were published. From Afghanistan to Yugoslavia, this bibliography has compiled a wealth of historical resources in a single volume.

Dictionaries and Encyclopedias

165. Altbach, Philip G., ed. **International Higher Education: An Encyclopedia**. New York: Garland, 1991. 2 vol. (*Garland Reference Library of the Social Sciences* v. 506). $60.00. LC: 90-46952. ISBN: 0-8240-4847-4.

   Sixteen topical areas provide the framework for this encyclopedia and overview of the status and trends within higher education. The sixteen areas include issues of accountability, governance, academic freedom, students, and the history of higher education. In addition, articles on the current status of higher education within fifty-one countries in seven geographic regions are presented. Written by international scholars, these entries provide factual information as well as insights into the system and are supported by references. A bibliography; list of contributors; and indexes to subjects, names, and locations are provided. Valuable information about international higher education is supplied within this two volume encyclopedia.

166.   Clark, Burton R., and Neave, Guy, ed. **Encyclopedia of Higher Education**. Oxford, Eng.: Pergamon, 1992. 4 vol. $1,250.00. ISBN: 0-08-037251-1.

Organized thematically into four volumes, the encyclopedia presents an alphabetical list by country of 138 national systems of higher education in the first volume. Analytical perspectives on higher education and society; the institutional fabric of the system; governance, administration, and finance; faculty and students; and disciplinary perspectives appear in the second and third volumes. The fourth volume offers articles about the status of the academic disciplines (humanities, social sciences, biological sciences, medical sciences, and physical sciences) as well as thorough name and subject indexes. An international complement of contributors are responsible for the contents, supported by references for each article, in all areas of the encyclopedia. This is a quality resource for international higher education research. Also available as *Education: The Complete Encyclopedia (CD-ROM)* issued on the same CD-ROM with *International Encyclopedia of Education.*

167.   Knowles, Asa S., ed. **International Encyclopedia of Higher Education**. San Francisco: Jossey-Bass, 1977. 10 vol. $800.00. LC: 77-73647. ISBN: 0-87589-323-6.

Two decades since its publication, this encyclopedia still offers useful information about higher education in an international context. While many global changes have made some of the entries obsolete, there is still a historical perspective to be gained from the content of this reference source. Contents include descriptions of education systems in 198 countries and territories; topical essays addressing politics, economics, historical perspectives, and more in higher education; descriptions of 142 fields of study; listings of educational associations, research centers and institutes; education reports; a glossary; and, a list of international acronyms. An entire volume is devoted to name and subject indexes. This is a valuable source of standard information related to higher education.

168. Nicolescu, Adrian, ed. **Multilingual Lexicon of Higher Education**. Munchen, Germany: K. G. Saur, 1995. 2 vol. $200.00. ISBN: 3-598-10883-4. Sponsored by CEPES, UNESCO.

Volume 1 of this set includes Western Europe and North America; volume 2 includes eastern and southeastern Europe and Israel. Countries are listed alphabetically within each volume. Each entry is divided into nine categories that allow for comparison between different systems. The terms are listed in the language of the country, however, the definitions are provided in English. A list of abbreviations is provided in each volume, as are select bibliographies and country indexes. The country indexes highlight terms used in each country and indicate where the definition may be found within the volume. Useful to those seeking comparisons between different systems of education, clarification of terminology, and comparison of degrees and their equivalency.

Directories and Almanacs

169. **American Universities and Colleges**. 15th ed. New York: Walter de Gruyter, 1997. 1,841 p. $199.95. ISSN: 0066-0922. ISBN: 3-11-014689-4.

Produced in collaboration with the American Council on Education and originally published in 1928, this directory now includes more than 1,900 institutions offering baccalaureate or higher degrees. The directory segment provides standard information about each institution, including enrollment, accreditation, history, governance, admissions, degree requirements, costs, financial aid, student body characteristics, student life, facilities, and specific programs. Prefatory material includes overviews of the history of higher education and its current structure and status in the U.S. Professional education, its accreditation, and accredited programs are covered. Includes indexes by institution and a brief general index.

170. Anaya, Alison, ed. **Accredited Institutions of Postsecondary Education, Programs, Candidates 1996-97**. Phoenix, Ariz.: Oryx Press, 1997. 735 p. $54.95. LC: 81-641495. ISSN: 0270-1715. ISBN: 1-57356-030-8. Copyrighted by the American Council on Education.

Listing accredited institutions and programs in higher education, this guide offers the prospective student some assurance of the credibility of a degree. Acknowledging that not all disciplines have recognized professional accreditation and that some institutions have specific programs that are not accredited, while other programs may have accreditation, this authoritative work provides information in one accessible source. Provided are lists of accrediting bodies, accredited degree-granting and non-degree granting institutions (primarily in the U.S.), and a list of candidate institutions on the path to accreditation. A list of public systems of higher education, as well as a description of the accrediting process are included.

171. Atwell, Robert H., and Pierce, David. **American Community Colleges: A Guide**. 10th ed. Phoenix, Ariz.: Oryx Press, 1995. 909 p. (*American Council on Education/Oryx Press Series on Higher Education*). $135.00. ISSN: 1079-7599. ISBN: 0-89774-874-3.

Organized alphabetically by state and city, this directory provides descriptive information for community colleges throughout the U.S. and its territories. Each entry provides contact information; general background information including type of control and accreditation; academic information such as admission requirements, calendar, areas of study, enrollment, staffing, and student life; and financial costs and aid. Lengthy and thorough indexes by field of study and institution name are provided. A quality publication for information about community colleges and courses of study. Former title *American Community, Technical, and Junior Colleges: A Guide.*

172. Bauer, David G. **The Complete Grants Sourcebook for Higher Education**. 3rd ed. Phoenix, Ariz.: Oryx, 1996. 340 p. (*American Council on Education/Oryx Press Series on Higher Education*). $85.00. LC: 95-47018. ISBN: 0-89774-821-2.

The sourcebook contains information about the process for writing successful grant applications, and a directory to foundation, corporate, and government sources of funding. The directory sections provide addresses, areas of interest or specialization including restrictions, application procedures, and sample grants that have been awarded. Indexes by subject, funding agencies by state and name, federal programs, and additional foundations of potential interest greatly enhance the usefulness of this directory and guide.

173. Bowman, J. Wilson. **America's Black and Tribal Colleges**. South Pasadena, Calif.: Sandcastle Publishing, 1994. 307 p. $21.95. LC: 94-66573. ISBN: 1-883995-02-7.

Directed to a very specific audience, this readable guide to historically and predominantly Black and American Indian colleges and universities offers brief historical background about each college, a chronology of name changes, a profile of the institution and its academic programs, fees, and a list of distinguished alumni. While each school entry is brief, it appeals to the student seeking information and discusses the advantages of attending one. Appendixes list colleges alphabetically by state, church, athletic affiliation, and those supported by the United Negro College Fund. A quick guide to scholarships is appended. General guidance regarding admission and financial aid appears in the prefatory matter of this useful and focused directory.

174.   **College Blue Book**. 26th ed. New York: Simon & Schuster Macmillan, 1997. 5 vol. $340.50. ISSN: 1082-7064. ISBN: 0-02-864758-0.

Published since 1923, and now issued in five volumes, the *College Blue Book* provides information to the college applicant in a variety of formats. Volume 1 provides a narrative description of the approximately 3,000 U.S. and Canadian colleges included. Each entry includes contact information, entrance requirements, costs, and the college and community environment. Volume 2 indicates costs, accreditation, enrollment, faculty, facilities, calendar system, names of admissions contacts, and more in tabular form. Volume 3 lists the programs offered by each college under the name of the institution in one part, while the second part lists the degrees offered and indicates which colleges have those programs. Volume 4 is focused on occupational education programs in nearly 7,100 business, trade, and technical schools. An alphabetical listing by state is provided with each entry indicating contact information, costs, enrollment, type of degree or certificate awarded, accreditation, and the curriculum. Ranging from medical technicians to flight personnel, the schools listed here offer a wide array of educational training opportunities. The latter half of this volume has a list arranged by the curricula and program being offered by each school, thus providing subject access. Volume 5 is the financial information part of this set, focusing on scholarships, fellowships, grants and loans. Organized according to field of study such as general, environmental studies, humanities, and so on, this volume provides information about funding sources in each category. Each entry provides the name and contact information for the funding agency; the area it is designated for; level of education for which award is granted; number, type, and amount of awards; eligibility requirements; application deadlines and procedures; and additional information. Indexes by subject, level of education, sponsoring organization, and title of award greatly enhance access to funding information. This combined set is a valuable addition to any collection offering educational opportunity and funding resource information to its students, faculty and staff, and other clientele.

175. Doughty, Harold R. **Guide to American Graduate Schools**. 8th ed. New York: Penguin Books, 1997. 635 p. $24.95. ISBN: 0-14-046986-9.

    More than 1,200 institutions offering graduate or professional programs in the U.S. are described. With an introduction that offers a brief history of graduate education and professional schools, selection of a program of study, admission issues, and financial assistance, this guide offers more than a simple listing of programs. Each entry includes general institutional information, including tuition; graduate program requirements and offerings; admission requirements and standards; financial aid; degree requirements; fields of study; and, when available, housing and research facilities. Indexes include location of institutions by state, institutional abbreviations, and fields of study.

176. Drozdowski, Mark J., and Cullen, Patrick. **Insider's Guide to Graduate Programs in Education**. Boston: Allyn and Bacon, 1997. 175 p. $19.95. ISBN: 0-205-19511-3.

    Offers practical and experienced guidance to individuals considering graduate work in education. The introduction presents issues for consideration when contemplating graduate studies, an overview of graduate schools in education and their unique nature, and current issues and trends in graduate education, particularly teacher education and education reform. A state-by-state directory of graduate programs in education follows. Each entry includes basic data, including address, enrollments, programs offered, and tests required, among others. Also provided are addresses for state offices of certification and an index by specific programs.

177. Edwards, Alan F., Jr. **Interdisciplinary Undergraduate Programs: A Directory**. 2nd ed. Acton, Mass.: Copley Publishing Group, 1996. 435 p. $39.95. ISBN: 0-87411-881-6.

    Sponsored by the Association for Integrative Studies, this directory provides descriptions of 410 interdisciplinary programs at institutions of higher education in the U.S. Each entry includes the type of interdisciplinary program, courses, administration, narrative, and contact information. Appendixes provide listings by state and institution, by program type, and a copy of the questionnaire used to gather data.

178. Fiske, Edward B., and Logue, Robert. **Fiske Guide to Colleges 1999**. 15th ed. New York: Random House, 1999. 747 p. $20.00. ISBN: 0-8129-3005-3.

This is a selective guide to approximately 300 colleges and universities in the U.S. Rather than a comprehensive listing, high profile public and private institutions are featured in essays describing their academic and social settings. Each essay describes academics, campus setting, student body, financial aid, housing, food, social life, and extracurricular activities. Statistics on enrollment, test scores, acceptance rates and scores for the quality of programs are provided in sidebars. Indexes by state, name of institution, and cost are included. The best values for college attendance are also noted with special graphics. Offers insights into "the best and most interesting" colleges that were selected for inclusion.

179. **International Handbook of Universities**. 15th ed. Paris: International Association of Universities, 1998. 2,474 p. $245.00. ISBN: 1-56159-222-6.

Published since 1959, the *Handbook* provides listings for more than 6,000 universities in 174 countries and territories. Each entry includes the title of the institution, address and contact information and, when available, listings of the departments, academic year, admission requirements, costs, degrees offered, language of instruction, number of staff, and student enrollment. Some entries are very brief while others are quite extensive. Entries are arranged alphabetically by country and institution. An index to institution names is also provided. Helpful source of information about universities worldwide.

180. Mitchell, Robert. **Multicultural Student's Guide to Colleges: What Every African-American, Asian-American, Hispanic and Native American Applicant Needs to Know About America's Top Schools**. Rev. ed. New York: Noonday Press, 1996. 745 p. $25.00. LC: 93-21749. ISBN: 0-374-52476-9.

Excellent source of information about colleges for students of color. Brief introductory sections discuss the application process and financial aid. Over 200 colleges and universities are described with comments from attending students, and factual information such as cost, number of non-white students enrolled, retention rate of students of color, remediation programs, relevant student organizations, and notable alumni of color. Separate listings are provided of U.S. predominantly Black colleges and universities, Native American colleges, and Hispanic-serving colleges and universities.

181. **National Faculty Directory 1999**. 29th ed. Detroit, Mich.: Gale, 1998. 3 vol. $730.00. LC: 76-14404. ISSN: 0077-4472.

Indispensable aid to locating more than 670,000 teaching faculty at over 3,600 American community colleges, colleges, and universities, and at 240 English-oriented Canadian institutions. Only teaching faculty are included with name, academic department, institution, and postal address. A separate section at the beginning of each volume lists the colleges and universities included with a mailing address and general telephone number. Data is drawn from current class schedules and academic catalogs, and is updated annually. Also available electronically.

182.   **NEA Almanac of Higher Education**. Washington, D.C.: National Education Association, 1996. 193 p. ISSN: 0743-670X.

The almanac consists of essays that provide an overview on the current state of higher education and statistical reports in key areas, such as faculty salaries. Essays cover current issues such as faculty workload, accountability, faculty governance, and increasing administrative layers in the university. Produced by the National Education Association, this almanac offers an annual view of key and often controversial topics within higher education.

183.   **Peterson's Annual Guides to Graduate Study**. 33rd ed. Princeton, N.J.: Peterson's, 1999. 6 vol. $193.70. ISSN: 1088-9442.

This set of annual guides is the foremost publication of its kind, providing information about graduate and professional programs at accredited institutions in the U.S. and abroad. Divided into six volumes, each available separately, they are organized as follows: Book 1, an overview; Book 2, humanities, arts and social sciences; Book 3, biological sciences; Book 4, physical sciences, mathematics, agricultural sciences, environment, and natural resources; Book 5, engineering and applied sciences; and, Book 6, business, education, health, information studies, law and social work. Each individual volume lists institutions offering programs in the areas designated. The descriptions may be lengthy, if supplied by the institution, or relatively brief if part of the standard format supplied by the publisher. All institutions are included in the standard descriptions with cross-references to institutionally-supplied descriptions. Each includes contact information, fields of study, accreditation, admissions information, degree requirements, costs, and financial aid information. Indexes are provided for those promotional descriptions supplied by institutions, for the subject fields covered by all the volumes in the set, and for the subject fields contained in the volume at hand. This publication should be a standard resource in any institution serving the needs of undergraduate students and others interested in graduate study.

184. **Peterson's Internships 1999**. 19th ed. Princeton, N.J.: Peterson's, 1998. 676 p. $24.95. ISSN: 1082-2577. ISBN: 0-7689-0044-1.

Subtitled "More Than 50,000 Opportunities to Get an Edge in Today's Competitive Job Market," this directory lists internship opportunities by the type of sponsoring business or organization offering it. These categories include hospitality and travel, arts and entertainment, educational services, finance and insurance, health care and social services, information services, manufacturing, real estate, and professional or legal services. Each entry provides a description, contact information, available internships, eligibility requirements, benefits, duration, location of placement, and eligibility for college credit. Indexes provide access by field of interest, geographic location, international internships, employer, academic level required, international applicant acceptance, paid internships, and potential for permanent employment. Useful resource for high school through graduate students and others interested in internship opportunities.

185. **Peterson's Register of Higher Education**. 10th ed. Princeton, N.J.: Peterson's, 1997. 1,158 p. $49.95. ISSN: 1046-2406. ISBN: 1-56079-658-8.

Listing administrative officers with telephone numbers is one of the unique features of this directory. While other directories may include similar information about institutions of higher education regarding institutional address, telephone and FAX numbers, type, accreditation, enrollment, and possibly names of major administrators, few offer direct telephone listings for those administrators. In some instances, names and telephone numbers of heads of major academic units are also provided. Indexes provide additional access points by major academic units within institutions, administrative officers and academic unit heads, specialized and professional accreditation, and geographical location. Appendixes list federal and state higher education offices, accrediting agencies, higher education associations, and higher education consortia. Introductory essays by leaders within higher education provide a framework for the state of higher education in the U.S. This is a helpful resource for anyone trying to track down the current upper level personnel in institutions of higher education.

186. Rich, Elizabeth H., ed. **National Guide to Funding in Higher Education**. 5th ed. New York: Foundation Center, 1998. 1,439 p. $145.00. ISBN: 0-87954-771-5.

One of several funding directories from the Foundation Center, this one focuses on foundation, corporate, and other charitable support for higher education. Over 4,800 foundations are listed with basic information, including address, assets, expenditures, types of support provided, limitations, application information, and recent grants awarded. Six indexes provide access by names of donors, officers, and trustees; geographic location; type of support; grant maker by subject, grants by subject; and, name of grant maker.

187. Rodenhouse, Mary Pat, ed. **HEP . . . Higher Education Directory**. 16th ed. Falls Church, Va.: Higher Education Publications, 1998. 636 p. $52.00. LC: 83-641119. ISSN: 0736-0797. ISBN: 0-914927-25-6.

Published since 1983, the *HEP Directory* provides quick, accurate data regarding accredited postsecondary degree-granting institutions in the United States. Using geographical organization, institutions are listed within each state alphabetically. In addition to address, telephone, FAX, URL, Carnegie classification, calendar system, date of establishment, enrollment, affiliation (if any), accreditation, highest degree offered, and program focus, the FICE number (needed for student financial aid applications) is readily provided. Chief officers and deans of major programs are listed by title and name. Additional sections provide lists of accrediting agencies, acronyms, statewide agencies of higher education, higher education associations, higher education consortia, and religious affiliation by denomination. As a ready source of information about higher education institutions, this is an excellent resource.

188. Schlachter, Gail Ann, and Weber, R. David. **Financial Aid for Native Americans, 1997-1999**. El Dorado Hills, Calif.: Reference Service Press, 1997. 616 p. (*Minority Funding Set*). $37.50. ISBN: 0-918276-59-4. Formerly *Directory of Financial Aids for Minorities,* issued in four volumes.

One of several guides to financial aid for special populations from this publisher, this directory lists funding resources for Native Americans. Populations that would benefit from resources listed are American Indians, Native Alaskans, Native Pacific Islanders, and Native Americans in general. Arranged by type of funding and category of targeted audience, this directory offers thorough information for financial assistance for education, research, travel, and professional development. Funding sources provide support to individuals from high school to postsecondary levels. An annotated bibliography of general financial aid books is provided, as are a series of indexes to provide access by program title, subject, sponsoring agency, residency, tenability, and deadlines. Issued biennially. Other reference sources from this publisher include financial aid books targeted to African Americans, Asian Americans, Hispanic Americans, women, individuals with disabilities, and veterans or military personnel.

189. Vuturo, Christopher. **The Scholarship Advisor 1999**. New York: Princeton Review, 1998. 835 p. $23.00. ISBN: 0-375-75207-2.

Offering practical guidance and sample forms for applying for scholarships, this directory includes specialized indexes such as name of scholarship, academic interests, career interests, college, ethnic, disabilities, and religious affiliation. The scholarship entries are written in tabular form with contact information, award type, level of study, amount, deadline, and eligibility requirements. Suitable for both undergraduate and graduate student scholarships and packed with information, the guide would have been improved by an expanded table of contents listing the location of the fourteen specialized indexes buried in the scholarship locator chapter.

190. Wood, Donna, ed. **Research Centers Directory 1999**. 24th ed. Detroit: Gale, 1998. 2 vol. $530.00. ISSN: 0278-2731. ISBN: 0-7876-2195-1.

Approximately 14,100 research centers are described and listed in this directory. Included are nonprofit research centers, institutes, operating foundations, laboratories, bureaus, experiment stations, and other research facilities. Volume 1 includes descriptions of centers in five broad categories: life sciences; physical sciences and engineering; private and public policy and affairs; social and cultural studies; and multidisciplinary and research coordinating centers. Volume 2 provides four indexes by name of organization, personal name, geographical location, and subject. Each entry describes the mission of the center, its budget, staffing, and outreach efforts. This is a specialized directory of interest to researchers, scholars and students. Also available electronically.

191. **The World of Learning**. 47th ed. London: Europa Publications Limited, 1997. 2,026 p. $445.00. LC: 47-30172. ISSN: 0084-2117. ISBN: 1-85743-032-8.

Using a geographic arrangement by country, this massive directory provides basic address information for learned societies, research institutes, libraries and archives, and museums and art galleries. More detailed information is provided about universities in each country, often including faculty within academic departments. A brief section on international organizations, such as UNESCO, and the International Association of Universities precedes the country listings. With its annual updates, this directory provides current, comprehensive information about institutions of higher education around the globe. An index by institution title provides added access points.

Guides, Handbooks, and Yearbooks

192.   British Council, National Academic Recognition Information Centre for the United Kingdom (NARIC). **International Guide to Qualifications in Education**. 4th ed. London: Mansell Publishing Ltd., 1996. 919 p. $200.00. LC: 95-18218. ISBN: 0-7201-2217-1.

Written for the United Kingdom, this guide to educational credentials will nonetheless be useful for admissions officers in other countries attempting to determine the level of achievement of individuals from 165 countries. Each entry describes the educational system, its levels, marking systems, certificates and diplomas, and further and higher education. Appendixes provide information about degrees and certificates from specific geographic regions, such as the West African Examinations Council.

193.   **A Classification of Institutions of Higher Education**. Princeton, N.J.: Carnegie Foundation for the Advancement of Teaching , 1994. 168 p. (*A Technical Report*). $15.00. LC: 94-36243. ISBN: 0-931050-46-4. Foreword by Ernest L. Boyer.

Using a classification system developed by Clark Kerr in 1970, this report clusters U.S. colleges and universities according to their missions. Definitions of each of the classifications (Research I, Doctoral II, Baccalaureate Colleges II, Specialized Institutions, and so on) are provided, as are lists of each institution so categorized. The index makes it extremely simple for a researcher to determine an institution's classification. The foreword by Boyer gives an overview of the history of the classification scheme and its current status, and tables show the changes that have occurred in enrollment patterns by type of institution over nearly 20 years.

194.   **College Catalog Collections on Microfiche**. San Diego, Calif.: Career Guidance Foundation, 1973-. 3 updates per year. price varies. ISSN: 0733-1355.

The college catalog collection produced on microfiche provides a space-saving option for those institutions wishing to provide current information about course offerings from institutions of higher education. Only those institutions recognized as accredited by the U.S. Department of Education are included. Approximately 3,000 colleges and universities are represented. Most institutions are from the U.S., but selected international colleges and universities are included as well. Updates to the collection are issued three times annually, and include summer as well as annual catalogs. A paper index to the collection is provided.

195. College Entrance Examination Board. **College Handbook 1999**. New York: College Board, 1998. 1,623 p. $25.95. LC: 41-12971. ISBN: 0-87447-590-2.

Issued with the *College Explorer* CD-ROM, this guide provides descriptions of 3,200 U.S. colleges with forty indexes to provide access by a variety of characteristics. The CD-ROM includes Internet links to college home pages when available. Prefatory material includes guidance about college selection and admissions processes. The descriptions are subdivided by two-year and four-year institutions, each including general information, class profiles, costs, application procedures, majors, athletics, and student life and services. A comprehensive source at a reasonable price.

196. Danesy, Frank C. **Higher Education Credentials: A Guide to Educational Systems in Europe and North America**. New York: John Wiley & Sons, 1994. 176 p. $99.50. LC: 93-43238. ISBN: 0-471-94269-3.

Compiled to document the higher education credentials awarded in those countries that are part of the European Space Agency, this work focuses on the areas of engineering, mathematics, natural sciences, business administration, economics, and law, pivotal to the aerospace industry. Because of global participation in higher education and work, Canada and the United States are also included among the countries with credentials described. Listed under each country are the credentials awarded by universities and non-university institutions of higher education; the secondary school credentials required for admission to higher education programs, and a table listing the names of the various degrees, entrance requirements, and program length. Extremely useful guide for admissions officers working with international credentials.

197. Fitzpatrick, Jacqueline, Secrist, Jan, and Wright, Debra J. **Secrets for a Successful Dissertation**. Thousand Oaks, Calif.: Sage, 1998. 184 p. $40.00. LC: 98-8899. ISBN: 0-7619-1250-9.

Combining humor with pragmatism, the authors present a series of steps to cope with the rigorous demands of the dissertation process. From writing the proposal to dealing with writing blocks to defending the dissertation, each step is addressed. Emphasis is given to developing support groups, careful selection of advisors, and setting up reasonable schedules and expectations. Tips for success in the form of checklists are appended to each chapter. Appendixes offer useful terms for overworked phrases and verbs, a checklist for the research proposal, and a statistical decision tree. A bibliography of further readings and an index are included.

198.   Gourman, Jack. **The Gourman Report: A Rating of Graduate and Professional Programs in American and International Universities**. 8th, rev. ed. New York: Princeton Review, 1997. 302 p. $21.95. ISBN: 0-679-78374-1.

Although the Gourman reports remain controversial, based on the lack of clearly stated criteria for rankings and inclusion, they remain very popular with consumers. This is particularly true because few other rankings guides list as many programs of study. The graduate programs volume includes ranked listings of general graduate programs, law schools, medical schools, health programs, engineering programs, business schools, doctoral programs in management, and leading international universities. The author does not approve of graduate schools of education or criminal justice/criminology correction programs based on his characterization of them as below average. Given the popular but controversial nature of this source, readers should consult other print and Web-based rankings tools for more information.

199.   Gourman, Jack. **The Gourman Report: A Rating of Undergraduate Programs in American and International Universities**. 10th ed. New York: Princeton Review, 1997. 398 p. $21.95. ISBN: 0-679-77780-6.

Ranking over 140 fields of study, the Gourman report on undergraduate programs provides an evaluation of institutions, programs, administrative and support areas within universities, and international universities. In keeping with the author's stated views, rankings of undergraduate programs in criminal justice, forensic science, and education are not included because he does not approve of them. The introduction indicates that specific information about the data used to rank institutions and programs are included in the appendixes, however, the information is relatively vague. This is a popular tool, frequently requested by consumers. Given the lack of clarity in the evaluation process, users should be advised to use this source in conjunction with other print and Web-based rankings tools.

200.   **Index of Majors and Graduate Degrees 1999**. New York: College Board, 1998. 699 p. $18.95. LC: 80-648202. ISBN: 0-87447-592-9.

Over 600 majors are listed in this guide, representing nearly 3,000 accredited institutions. From the associate to the doctorate and professional degree, each major listed includes those institutions which offer an accredited degree in that area. Special academic programs that offer combined degrees, accelerated programs, distance learning options, and others are listed as well. A list of colleges represented in this book is included with zip codes. Complete address information must be obtained through other sources.

201. Kaplin, William A., and Lee, Barbara A. **The Law of Higher Education: A Comprehensive Guide to Legal Implications of Administrative Decision Making**. 3rd ed. San Francisco: Jossey-Bass, 1995. 1,023 p. (*Jossey-Bass Higher and Adult Education Series*). $75.00. LC: 94-38999 ISBN: 0-7879-0052-4.

This is an excellent source of understandable information about laws affecting higher education. Limited use of legal jargon and thorough indexing provide a reference source that is accessible to all, but written for the particular needs of administrative officers of colleges and universities. Divided into nine areas, each with an annotated bibliography, topics of particular concern are addressed. These nine areas are an overview of postsecondary law; trustees, administrators, and staff; faculty; students; community; state government; federal government; education associations; and, business/industrial community. From patent law to the immigration status of students, this guide addresses the issues and provides direction. In addition to a subject index, case and statute indexes are provided.

202. Leider, Anna J., ed. **The A's and B's of Academic Scholarships**. 20th ed. Alexandria, Va.: Octameron Associates, 1998. 204 p. $8.00. ISBN: 1-57509-033-3.

This guide to academic scholarships for students with a grade B average or higher offers advice and guidance in an easy-to-read format. The bulk of the text provides a chart with awards from over 1,000 colleges. The chart includes the type of award program, number of awards, monetary value, award criteria, and restrictions. Of greatest use to first-time college applicants, but applicable to anyone seeking financial aid for higher education.

203. Mauch, James E., and Birch, Jack W. **Guide to the Successful Thesis and Dissertation: A Handbook for Students and Faculty**. 4th ed. New York: Marcel Dekker, 1998. 335 p. $59.75. ISBN: 0-8247-0169-0.

Directed to advisors and students undertaking thesis or dissertation work, this practical guide should be required reading for everyone involved in the process. From beginning the process to completing the dissertation or thesis, each step is explained and pitfalls are highlighted. The fourth edition gives attention to intellectual property rights, confidentiality issues, use of research animals, and the incorporation of technology in the research process. A summary of each chapter is presented, and appendixes include a glossary of computer terms, suggested proposal guidelines, and a course outline for the advisor. A bibliography and author and subject indexes are also provided.

204. Summerfield, Carol, and Devine, Mary Elizabeth, ed. **International Dictionary of University Histories**. Chicago: Fitzroy Dearborn Publishers, 1998. 780 p. $125.00. ISBN: 1-884964-23-0.

Beginning with a historical overview of the university movement, this dictionary proceeds to individual descriptions of over 200 institutions around the globe. These institutions represent universities, colleges, and research centers that fulfill a diverse array of needs, such as land grant universities, special populations, language specialties, and so on. Each entry includes a history of the institution, a description, contact information, and the current role and importance of the institution. If available, English language university histories are listed for further information.

Indexes and Abstracts

205. **Higher Education Abstracts**. Claremont, Calif.: Claremont Graduate University, 1984-. v. 33, 1998. $195.00 institutions; $95.00 individuals. ISSN: 0748-4364. Volumes 1-19 published as *College Student Personnel Abstracts*.

Focuses on current research and theory related to higher education. Abstracted are scholarly journal articles, conference papers, and published or unpublished monographs and reports. The arrangement is by categories: students, faculty, administration, and higher education. Each category is subdivided so that all articles on a particular topic, such as faculty promotion and tenure, are clustered together. In addition to this topical arrangement reflected in the table of contents, separate author and subject indexes are provided. Valuable quarterly abstracting service.

206. **Research into Higher Education Abstracts**. Abingdon, Oxfordshire, Eng.: Carfax, 1966-. v. 31, 1998. 3 issues per year. $438.00 (institutions). ISSN: 0034-5326.

Published on behalf of the Society for Research into Higher Education, this abstracting service provides indexing to and abstracting of journals, books, and monographs related to higher education. The focus is on the United Kingdom and European higher education literature, with some coverage of other areas of the world, including the U.S. Abstracts are divided into eight key areas addressing national systems and comparative studies; institutional management; curriculum; research; students; staff; finance and physical resources; and, contributory studies and research approaches. Subject and author indexes offer detailed access, and a list of journals covered is provided. Useful for the research collection with a strong U.K. or European focus in higher education.

Statistical Sources

207. **Almanac of Higher Education 1995**. Chicago: University of Chicago Press, 1995. 390 p. $18.95. ISSN: 1044-3096. ISBN: 0-226-18460-9.

Prepared by the editors of the *Chronicle of Higher Education*, the almanac consists of charts, tables, and maps illustrating statistical trends in higher education. A section on sources and notes indicates the sources used for compiling data. The 1995 edition includes summary statistics on students, faculty and staff, resources, institutions, special international statistics, the states, and enrollment by race. The table of contents must be used in lieu of an index. There is little context for the statistical tables other than the title of each, however, the data is useful and compiled from reliable sources.

208. Andersen, Charles J. **Fact Book on Higher Education 1997**. Phoenix, Ariz.: American Council on Education and the Oryx Press, 1998. 254 p. (*Series on Higher Education*). $49.95. ISSN: 0363-6720. ISBN: 0-89774-820-4.

Using data from government agencies as well as nongovernmental sources, the *Fact Book* provides statistical information about trends within higher education. Divided into four categories, Demographic and Economic Data; Enrollment Data; Institution and Finance, Faculty, Staff and Students; and Earned Degrees, substantial information is provided for researchers seeking information about changes over time in these areas. Each of the four sections is preceded by a brief "highlights" section that points out significant changes in that category. For example, the Demographic and Economic Data section is preceded by brief statistical reports on the status of minorities and women in higher education. Each table within the *Fact Book* is accompanied by a graphic display of the data. A guide to sources at the end of the book identifies the major sources of data used. The sources are also indicated at the bottom of each table. The inclusion of an index and a descriptive table of contents makes this a particularly useful source of higher education data.

209.   Goldberger, Marvin L., Maher, Brendan A., and Flattau, Pamela Ebert, ed. **Research-Doctorate Programs in the United States: Continuity and Change**. Washington, D.C.: National Academy Press, 1995. 740 p. $59.95. LC: 95-35154. ISBN: 0-309-05094-4.

Conducted by the National Research Council, the research on which the contents of this work is based is considered to be of the highest quality. Rather than a popular approach to ranking doctoral programs, this project undertook careful examination of a number of factors including descriptive statistics and peer assessment of programs in order to compile evaluative information about 41 fields of study. The sources of information were over 3,600 programs at more than 270 institutions. Included are the background information and methodology of the study, selected findings, and summary information. Appendixes include specific findings and are available electronically. An index provides access to specific components of the 41 fields of study. Excellent source of reputable evaluation information.

210.   Phillipe, Kent A., ed. **National Profile of Community Colleges: Trends and Statistics 1997-1998**. Washington, D.C.: Community College Press, 1997. 116 p. $10.00. ISSN: 1083-2882. Continues: *Community, Technical, and Junior College Statistical Yearbook.*

Statistical data related to community colleges in the United States is presented through charts and tables. Six key areas are presented with brief overviews, followed by statistical data. These areas are basic demographic information about community colleges, student characteristics and enrollment, impact of community colleges, student costs and financial aid, institutional revenues, expenditures and staff, and the future of community colleges. A glossary defines the terms in order to better understand how they are applied. A list of references and electronic data sources is also provided in this excellent compilation of statistics about community colleges.

211.   Touchton, Judith G., and Davis, Lynne. **Fact Book on Women in Higher Education**. New York: American Council on Education and Macmillan, 1991. 289 p. $39.95. LC: 90-20408. ISBN: 0-02-900951-0.

The introduction to this statistical source sets the context in which the data is presented. Highlights and trends are noted in brief narrative passages that are followed by tables, graphs, and charts of statistical information related to the status of women within higher education. This information is categorized as demographic and economic data, high school and the transition to higher education, enrollment, earned degrees, administrators, trustees and staff, and student aid. A final section provides information about the sources used to compile the data, with accompanying tables of information. A bibliography is provided as is an index to the contents of this statistical compendium drawn from reputable sources.

World Wide Web and Internet Sources

212. **College and University Home Pages**. http://www.mit.edu:8001/people/cdemello/univ.html (accessed February 28, 1999).

An international list of home pages of colleges and universities is provided at this site. Access is by alphabetical or geographical lists to more than 3,000 institutions. Also included at this site are background information about the site, its contents, and limitations. As a way to quickly access the home pages of institutions worldwide, this is an excellent resource. It is easy to link to an institutional home page and then to the relevant department or service links provided by the university or college.

213. **College and University Rankings**. http://www.library.uiuc.edu/edx/rankings.htm (accessed February 26, 1999).

Developed as a tool for those seeking information about college and university rankings, this WWW resource offers links to rankings information in several categories, including general/undergraduate, graduate/research, business, law, and international programs. In addition to the annotated links, a list of print sources, a bibliography about rankings in general, and a caution and controversy statement are provided to offer a framework for rankings information. Due to the selective and evaluative nature of this Web site, it has received very positive reviews from several sources. Updated regularly.

Journals

214. **Academe: Bulletin of the American Association of University Professors**. Vol. 1-. Washington, D.C.: American Association of University Professors, 1915-. bimonthly. $60.00 (nonmembers). ISSN: 0190-2946.

One of the major sources of information on current issues within higher education, this AAUP publication offers informative articles and reports, regular columns on legislation, book reviews, and an annual salary report on the status of the profession. Indexed in: *Current Index to Journals in Education, Education Index, Higher Education Abstracts, Social Sciences Citation Index.*

215. **Black Issues in Higher Education**. Vol. 1-. Fairfax, Va.: Cox, Matthews & Associates, 1984-. 26 issues per year. $40.00. ISSN: 0742-0277.

Published every two weeks, this journal covers key issues within higher education as they affect African-Americans. Feature articles, news briefs, updates on new and pending legislation, and extensive job listings are included in each issue. Of interest to people of color and to those involved in studying higher education. Indexed in: *Current Index to Journals in Education, Education Index, Higher Education Abstracts.*

216. **Change: The Magazine of Higher Learning**. Vol. 1-. Washington, D.C.: Heldref, 1969-. bimonthly. $75.00 (institutions). ISSN: 0009-1383.

Published under the leadership of the American Association for Higher Education, this journal provides information on current issues and activities in higher education. Classroom concerns, institutional responsibilities, accreditation issues, and more are covered. Regular features include book reviews, brief updates on higher education news, and job advertisements. Indexed in: *Current Index to Journals in Education, Education Index, Educational Administration Abstracts, Higher Education Abstracts.*

217. **Chronicle of Higher Education**. Vol. 1-. Washington, D.C.: Chronicle of Higher Education, 1954-. weekly. $75.00. ISSN: 0009-5982.

Viewed as the major weekly newspaper in higher education, the *Chronicle* offers brief reports on a variety of topics as well as in-depth articles on key topics. Job listings are a popular feature because they cover all areas of higher education. Regular sections address faculty, students, research, information technology, government and politics, money and management, athletics, the international arena, and include an opinion and arts section. Also available electronically. Indexed in: *Current Index to Journals in Education.*

218. **College and University**. Vol. 1-. Washington, D.C.: American Association of Collegiate Registrars and Admissions Officers, 1925-. quarterly. $30.00 (nonmembers). ISSN: 0010-0889.

Specialized higher education journal that focuses on topics relevant to admissions officers and registrars. Research-based articles as well as practical implementation articles, book reviews, and opinion pieces are included. Indexed in: *Current Index to Journals in Education.*

219. **College Board Review**. Vol. 1-. New York: College Board, 1947-. quarterly. $25.00. ISSN: 0010-0951.

This College Board publication provides a forum for the topics of guidance, testing, financial aid, retention, and other areas of interest within higher education. Articles are generally essays and opinion pieces. Also includes book reviews. Indexed in: *Current Index to Journals in Education.*

220. **College Student Journal: A Journal Pertaining to College Students and Post-Secondary Instruction**. Vol. 1-. Mobile, Ala.: Project Innovation, 1967-. quarterly. $30.00 (institutions). ISSN: 0146-3934.

Includes research related to college students, their attitudes, opinions and values, as well as to instruction and instructional design, evaluation, and techniques in higher education. Many, but not all, contributions are authored by graduate students. Indexed in: *Higher Education Abstracts, Linguistics and Language Behavior Abstracts, Psychological Abstracts, Sociological Abstracts.*

221. **College Teaching**. Vol. 1-. Washington, D.C.: Heldref, 1953-. quarterly. $60.00 (institutions). ISSN: 8756-7555.

Includes articles that address teaching at the undergraduate and graduate levels, and that have an evaluative component. Practical articles focus on everything from classroom techniques to professional development. Indexed in: *Current Index to Journals in Education, Education Index, Research into Higher Education Abstracts, Sociology of Education Abstracts.*

222. **Community College Journal**. Vol. 1-. Washington, D.C.: American Association of Community Colleges, 1930-. bimonthly. $28.00 (nonmembers). ISSN: 1067-1803.

Association information, research articles, opinion pieces, and regular features such as book reviews and brief reports of legislation and current policy appear in this journal. Of interest to association members and to those concerned with community and junior college issues. Indexed in: *Current index to Journals in Education.*

223.   **Community College Journal of Research and Practice**. Vol.1-. London: Taylor & Francis, 1977-. 8 issues per year. $250.00 (institutions). ISSN: 1066-8926.

Research-based articles that address community and junior college education are the focus of this publication. Book reviews, listings of recent relevant dissertations, and a section of relevant ERIC reports are regular features. Indexed in: *Current Index to Journals in Education, Higher Education Abstracts.*

224.   **Community College Review**. Vol. 1-. Raleigh, N.C.: Department of Adult and Community College Education, School of Education, North Carolina State University, 1973-. quarterly. $55.00. ISSN: 0091-5521.

This refereed journal provides research-based articles on community college education. Experience-based articles are also presented if they address key issues within community colleges. Of particular interest to community college administrators and faculty. Indexed in: *Current Index to Journals in Education.*

225.   **Continuing Higher Education Review**. Vol. 1-. Cambridge, Mass.: Harvard University, 1937-. annual. $25.00. ISSN: 0893-0384.

Sponsored by the University Continuing Education Association and directed to higher education leaders and continuing education professionals, the contents of this annual publication include essays, association news and reports, and relevant book reviews. Indexed in: *Current Index to Journals in Education.*

226.   **CUPA Journal**. http://www.cupa.org/membonly/memberso.htm. Vol. 1-. Washington, D.C.: College and University Personnel Association, 1950-. 2 issues per year. $75.00 (institutions). ISSN: 1046-9508.

Available electronically and in print to members, the journal is directed to human resources managers in higher education. Two types of articles predominate in the journal: practical "how-to" articles and those dealing with overall issues and trends in human resource management in higher education. Association information is also included. Indexed in: *Current Index to Journals in Education, Education Index.*

227. **Higher Education Quarterly**. Vol. 1-. Oxford, Eng.: Blackwell, 1946-. quarterly. $229.00 (institutions). ISSN: 0951-5224.

Formerly *Universities Quarterly*, this publication is one of the Society for Research into Higher Education imprints. Research, essay and analytical articles addressing policy, management, and academic issues in higher education are included. The scope is international, although higher education articles from the United Kingdom and Europe predominate. Indexed in: *Education Index, Linguistics and Language Behavior Abstracts, Research into Higher Education Abstracts, Social Sciences Citation Index, Sociology of Education Abstracts.*

228. **Higher Education: The International Journal of Higher Education and Educational Planning**. Vol. 1-. Dordrecht, The Netherlands: Kluwer Academic, 1971-. 8 issues per year. $512.00 (institutions). ISSN: 0018-1560.

Research, analytical, and overview articles related to issues and problems in higher education are presented. International in focus, topics range from student issues and characteristics to the role of the academic within the institution. Book reviews are included. Indexed in: *British Education Index, Current Index to Journals in Education, Education Index, Educational Administration Abstracts, Higher Education Abstracts, Research into Higher Education Abstracts, Social Sciences Citation Index, Sociology of Education Abstracts.*

229. **Innovations in Education and Training International**. Vol. 1-. London: Routledge, 1964-. quarterly. $154.00 (institutions). ISSN: 1355-8005.

The official journal of the Staff and Educational Development Association includes research articles, case studies, and opinion papers. Focused on staff training and development in higher education, all relevant areas are covered. Indexed in: *British Education Index, Research into Higher Education Abstracts, Social Sciences Citation Index.*

230. **Innovative Higher Education**. Vol. 1-. New York: Human Sciences Press, 1976-. quarterly. $255.00 (institutions). ISSN: 0742-5627.

Scholarly articles that address both theory and practice appear in this journal devoted to innovations in higher education. Indexed in: *Current Index to Journals in Education, Education Index,*

Higher Education Abstracts, Psychological Abstracts, Sociological Abstracts.

231. **Journal of Blacks in Higher Education**. Vol. 1-. New York: CH II Publishers, 1993-. quarterly. $36.00. ISSN: 1077-3711.

   "Dedicated to the conscientious investigation of the status and prospects for African Americans in higher education," this quarterly publication provides a huge amount of information. Articles on current status, historical essays, reviews of books and scholarly research, grants, notable honors and awards, scholarly papers presented, appointments, tenure decisions and promotions, and reports of race relations on campus are featured in each issue. Valuable addition to any higher education collection. Indexed in: *Current Index to Journals in Higher Education, Higher Education Abstracts.*

232. **Journal of College and University Law**. Vol. 1-. Washington, D.C.: National Association of College and University Attorneys, 1971-. quarterly. $52.50. ISSN: 0093-8688.

   With contributors such as college and university counsel and education law specialists, the focus of this journal is on higher education legal concerns and issues. Contents include legislative and administrative developments, commentaries on recent cases, student comments, book reviews, and occasional association reports or papers. Indexed in: *Current Index to Journals in Education, Current Index to Legal Periodicals.*

233. **Journal of College Student Development**. Vol. 1-. Washington, D.C.: American College Personnel Association, 1960-. bimonthly. $45.00. ISSN: 0897-5264.

   Book reviews, brief research reports, quantitative and qualitative research articles, and essays related to student development appear in this journal. Student services, student and professional development, and administrative and professional issues are all presented in relation to the campus environment and student affairs. Former title *Journal of College Student Personnel.* Indexed in: *Current Index to Journals in Education, Education Index, Educational Administration Abstracts, Higher Education Abstracts, Psychological Abstracts, Social Sciences Citation Index.*

234. **Journal of Higher Education**. Vol. 1-. Columbus, Ohio: Ohio State University Press, 1930-. bimonthly. $82.00 (institutions). ISSN: 0022-1546.

With a scholarly focus, this journal includes research, technical, professional practice and policy papers, and literature and book
reviews. Athletics, faculty, governance, students and technology are
just some of the higher education topics covered. Indexed in:
*Current Index to Journals in Education, Education Index, Educa-
tional Administration Abstracts, Higher Education Abstracts, Social Sciences Citation Index.*

235. **Liberal Education**. Vol. 1-. Washington, D.C.: Association of
American Colleges and Universities, 1915-. quarterly. $42.00 (non-
members). ISSN: 0024-1822.

Thematic issues provide a framework for discussions of liberal education in the higher education setting. Issues pertaining to
the curriculum, governance, and accountability are considered.
Also includes association news. Indexed in: *Current Index to Journals in Education, Education Index, Higher Education Abstracts,
Research into Higher Education Abstracts, Social Sciences Citation Index, Sociology of Education Abstracts.*

236. **NACADA Journal: The Journal of the National Academic Advising Association**. Vol. 1-. Manhattan, Kans.: National Academic
Advising Association, 1981-. 2 issues per year. $30.00 (institu-
tions). ISSN: 0271-9517.

Research articles, book reviews, bibliographies, and practical
reports are featured in this higher education journal devoted to
academic advising. Topics include new technologies, advising specific populations, and evaluation tools. Indexed in: *Current Index
to Journals in Education.*

237. **NASPA Journal**. Vol. 1-. Washington, D.C.: National Association
of Student Personnel Administrators, 1963-. quarterly. $35.00.
ISSN: 0027-6021.

Research articles, essays, historical overviews, and practical
reports are the focus of this student affairs publication. Directed to
a generalist student affairs administrator audience rather than specialists in the student affairs segment of higher education, some
specialized articles are included when they have broad interest or
implications. Also includes book reviews. Indexed in: *Current
Index to Journals in Education, Education Index, Higher Education
Abstracts.*

238. **New Directions for Community Colleges**. Vol. 1-. San Francisco:
Jossey-Bass, 1973-. quarterly. (*Jossey-Bass Higher and Adult Education Series*). $107.00 (institutions). ISSN: 0194-3081.

Issued quarterly in thematic issues with monographic titles, this publication features topics of interest to community colleges. Recent issues addressed remedial education, technology, organizational change, proprietary schools, and service learning. Indexed in: *Current Index to Journals in Education, Education Index, Higher Education Abstracts, Social Sciences Citation Index.*

239.   **New Directions for Higher Education**. Vol. 1-. San Francisco: Jossey-Bass, 1973-. quarterly. $99.00 (institutions). LC: 0271-0560.

Part of the *Jossey-Bass Higher and Adult Education Series*, this quarterly publication has a thematic approach for each issue, with a separate title and editor. Covering issues within higher education ranging from student assessment to campus governance and leadership, the contents of this journal are in constant demand. Indexed in: *Current Index to Journals in Education, Education Index, Higher Education Abstracts, Psychological Abstracts, Social Sciences Citation Index.*

240.   **New Directions for Institutional Research**. Vol. 1-. San Francisco: Jossey-Bass, 1974-. quarterly. (*Jossey-Bass Higher and Adult Education Series*). $95.00 (institutions). ISSN: 0271-0579.

Another of the quality Jossey-Bass publications, this one focuses on institutional research. Thematic issues with monographic titles are issued quarterly. Recent issues include quality assurance, campus climate, funding, litigation, and rankings as they affect the higher education institution. Indexed in: *Current Index to Journals in Education, Education Index, Higher Education Abstracts, Multicultural Education Abstracts.*

241.   **New Directions for Student Services**. Vol. 1-. San Francisco: Jossey-Bass, 1978-. quarterly. $99.00 (institutions). ISSN: 0164-7970.

Directed to the student affairs administrator or practitioner, this quarterly publication provides thematic issues, each available with a separate monographic title. Recent issues covered topics such as affirmative action, Greek letter organizations, African American males and college success, and ethics. Indexed in: *Current Index to Journals in Education, Education Index, Higher Education Abstracts, Multicultural Education Abstracts, Psychological Abstracts, Sociology of Education Abstracts.*

242. **New Directions for Teaching and Learning**. Vol. 1-. San Francisco: Jossey-Bass, 1980-. quarterly. (*Jossey-Bass Higher and Adult Education Series*). $90.00 (institutions). ISSN: 0271-0633.

Dedicated to exploring teaching and learning in higher education, this series presents quarterly thematic issues, each with a separate monographic title. Theory, research, and practice articles focus on the direction and future of teaching and learning within higher education, and how these evolving changes can be transferred into other settings. Recent issues have addressed assessment, academic advising, classroom management, and ethical concerns within higher education. Indexed in: *Current Index to Journals in Education, Education Index, Higher Education Abstracts, Psychological Abstracts*.

243. **Planning for Higher Education**.   Vol. 1-. Ann Arbor, Mich.: Society for College and University Planning, 1970-. quarterly. $50.00. ISSN: 0736-0983.

Addressing issues of interest to higher education administrators, this journal focuses on planning and policy making. Topics include facilities, trademarks, strategic planning, quality assurance, funding, and faculty workload. Research articles, program descriptions, practice reports, and book reviews are presented. Indexed in: *Current Index to Journals in Education, Education Index, Higher Education Abstracts, Multicultural Education Abstracts*.

244. **Research in Higher Education**. Vol. 1-. New York: Human Sciences Press, 1973-. bimonthly. $325.00 (institutions). ISSN: 0361-0365.

Directed to higher education administrators, faculty, and student personnel specialists, this journal presents research articles and brief methodological reports in areas such as student characteristics and achievement, alumni relations, administration, faculty issues, curriculum and instruction, and recruitment, admissions, and retention. Indexed in: *Current Index to Journals in Education, Education Index, Educational Administration Abstracts, Higher Education Abstracts, Multicultural Education Abstracts, Psychological Abstracts, Research into Higher Education Abstracts, Social Sciences Citation Index, Sociology of Education Abstracts*.

245. **Review of Higher Education**. Vol. 1-. Baltimore, Md.: Johns Hopkins University Press, 1977-. quarterly. $97.00 (institutions). ISSN: 0162-5748.

Published for the Association for the Study of Higher Education (ASHE), this scholarly journal provides a forum for articles, reviews, and essays related to higher education. Book reviews and abstracts of papers presented at ASHE conferences are also included. Indexed in: *Current Index to Journals in Higher Education, Higher Education Abstracts, Multicultural Education Abstracts, Research into Higher Education Abstracts, Social Sciences Citation Index.*

246.   **Thought and Action**. Vol. 1-. Washington, D.C.: National Education Association (NEA), 1984-. 2 issues per year. $30.00 (institutions). ISSN: 0748-8475.

As NEA's higher education journal, *Thought & Action* offers a forum for essays, research articles, commentaries, and book reviews. All aspects of higher education are considered, but quality articles with controversial stances are encouraged. Indexed in: *Current Index to Journals in Education, Higher Education Abstracts.*

247.   **Times Higher Education Supplement**. Vol. 1-. London: Times Supplements Ltd., 1971-. weekly. $99.00. ISSN: 0049-3929.

Comparable to the *Chronicle of Higher Education,* this British weekly newspaper offers information about current issues within higher education, recent research, book reviews, legislation affecting higher education and job advertisements. Indexed in: *Education Index, Research into Higher Education Abstracts.*

5

MULTILINGUAL AND
MULTICULTURAL EDUCATION

Dictionaries and Encyclopedias

248.　Baker, Colin, and Jones, Sylvia Prys. **Encyclopedia of Bilingualism and Bilingual Education**. Clevedon, Eng.: Multilingual Matters, 1998. 758 p. $150.00. LC: 96-24015. ISBN: 1-85359-362-1.

　　　Divided into four sections, Individual Bilingualism, Languages in Society, Languages in Contact in the World (Language Maps of the World), and Bilingual Education, this encyclopedia offers very readable background information about bilingualism in the global community. Enhanced by colorful photographs and illustrations, sidebars that highlight particular concepts, and references to further reading, this work is more than a dry reference tool. It will be gratefully received by students, researchers, and instructors seeking information on topics ranging from code switching to the whole language approach. Extremely valuable in its content, the authors have provided insights into the cultural issues associated with bilingualism from a variety of perspectives. A glossary, bibliography, and indexes further enhance this work.

249.　Jones-Wilson, Faustine C., ed. **Encyclopedia of African-American Education**. Westport, Conn.: Greenwood Press, 1996. 575 p. $95.00. LC: 95-42918. ISBN: 0-313-28931-X.

　　　This work combines biographical entries with definitions and descriptions of key events, laws, and policies related to African-American education. As an overview of significant events, and as a quick reference to terms, the editors and contributors have provided a valuable source. Not only are standard terms such as "white flight," "historically Black land-grant colleges," and "Head Start," included, but terms such as "pushouts," and the "Comer process" also appear. With its inclusion of key legislation, primary players in African-American education, a selected bibliography and thorough index, this encyclopedia is a critical resource for the study of African-American education within the United States.

Directories and Almanacs

250. Washburn, David E., and Brown, Neil L. **The Multicultural Education Directory**. Philadelphia: Inquiry International, 1996. 265 p. $39.95. LC: 96-77220. ISBN: 0-9635521-3-9.

Using a typology of multicultural education developed by Christine E. Sleeter and Carl A. Grant, this directory provides a listing by state and district of those programs participating in different aspects of multicultural education. Full program descriptions are provided for most, but not all, of the districts and schools. These descriptions include number of years in operation, grade levels, number of students participating, social and school goals, curricular and instructional aims, cultural groups studied, and availability of locally produced materials. Many of these categories are cross-referenced and indexed in other chapters of the book. Narrowly focused but useful directory.

Guides, Handbooks, and Yearbooks

251. Banks, James A., and Banks, Cherry A. McGee. **Handbook of Research on Multicultural Education**. New York: Macmillan, 1995. 882 p. $75.00. LC: 94-28862. ISBN: 0-02-895797-0.

The editors have assembled an overview of multicultural education through a series of essays by over 60 contributors that address the history of multicultural education, research issues, ethnic groups in educational context, immigration, language issues, intergroup education, higher education, and international education. Whether addressing gender, ability, or ethnicity in multicultural education, this handbook with its extensive references will be valuable to practitioners, scholars, and researchers. A subject index provides access to the contents of the 47 chapters.

252. Mitchell, Bruce M., and Salsbury, Robert E. **Multicultural Education: An International Guide to Research, Policies and Programs**. Westport, Conn.: Greenwood Press, 1996. 383 p. $85.00. LC: 95-37337. ISBN: 0-313-28985-9.

Based on an international survey of multicultural education undertaken by the authors, this guide provides an overview of multicultural education efforts in 42 countries. Each country profile includes an often fascinating history of the educational system set in the broader social context, the structure of the system, current multicultural education efforts, and a brief summary. Valuable both as a historical overview of each country's educational system and its programmatic efforts to incorporate multicultural education.

Statistical Sources

253. Nettles, Michael T., and Perna, Laura W. **African American Education Data Book**. Fairfax, Va.: Frederick D. Patterson Research Institute, The College Fund/UNCF, 1997. 3 vol. $75.00.

Issued in three volumes, this data book compiles information about the education of African-Americans in a single source. Using data from a variety of governmental, institutional, and other sources, each volume has a distinct focus. Volume 1 addresses higher and adult education; volume 2 includes preschool through high school education; and volume 3 focuses on the transition from school to college and the transition from school to work. Information is primarily statistical in form.

World Wide Web and Internet Sources

254. **NCBE Web Site**. http://www.ncbe.gwu.edu/ (accessed February 27, 1999).

The National Clearinghouse for Bilingual Education (NCBE) provides this Web site, and is funded by the U.S. Department of Education's Office of Bilingual Education and Minority Languages Affairs. As part of its mission to address critical issues dealing with the education of linguistically and culturally diverse students in the U.S. and provide information for those working in foreign language programs, English as a second language programs, Head Start, Title I, migrant education, and adult education programs, NCBE offers publications, an electronic discussion group, and this site. State policies and information related to multicultural students, full text resources, and much more are available through this valuable Web site.

Journals

255. **Bilingual Research Journal**. Vol. 1-. Washington, D.C.: National Association for Bilingual Education, 1975-. quarterly. $125.00. ISSN: 0885-5072.

Focusing on bilingualism and schooling, this journal includes research articles, policy analyses, evaluation studies, book reviews, and case studies. Excellent forum for topics related to language minority students. Indexed in: *Current Index to Journals in Education, Linguistics and Language Behavior Abstracts, Sociological Abstracts*.

256. **ELT Journal**. Vol. 1-. Oxford, Eng.: Oxford University Press, 1947-. quarterly. $87.00 (institutions). ISSN: 0951-0893.

Directed to those involved in teaching English as a second or foreign language, this journal includes practical articles, research-based reports, book reviews, and essays. Coverage is international in scope. Indexed in: *Current Index to Journals in Education.*

257. **English for Specific Purposes** . Vol. 1-. Exeter, Eng.: Elsevier Science, 1980-. 3 issues per year. $345.00 (institutions). ISSN: 0889-4906.

Formerly *ESP Journal*, this publication provides research articles, conference reports, and textbook and book reviews dealing with the use of English for specific purposes. Topics include second language acquisition, measurement, and curriculum development in an international context. Indexed in: *Current Index to Journals in Education, Linguistics and Language Behavior Abstracts, Multicultural Education Abstracts.*

258. **Equity and Excellence in Education**. Vol. 1-. Westport, Conn.: Greenwood, 1963-. 3 issues per year. $75.00 (institutions). ISSN: 1066-5684.

Formerly *Integrateducation*, the new title reflects the journal's emphasis on describing or evaluating practices to attain equity and excellence in education at all levels. Topics addressed include gender equity in athletics or computer use, exploring cultural differences, desegregation, and multiculturalism. Indexed in: *Current Index to Journals in Education, Education Index, Educational Administration Abstracts.*

259. **IRAL: International Review of Applied Linguistics in Language Teaching**. Vol. 1-. Heidelberg, Germany: Julius Groos Verlag, 1963-. quarterly. $145.00. ISSN: 0019-042X.

Articles and book reviews related to applied and general linguistics are published in English, French, or German. Second language teaching and acquisition are strongly emphasized. Indexed in: *Current Index to Journals in Education, Education Index, Linguistics and Language Behavior Abstracts, Multicultural Education Abstracts, Psychological Abstracts, Social Sciences Citation Index.*

260. **Journal of Multilingual and Multicultural Development.** Vol. 1-. Clevedon, Eng.: Multilingual Matters, 1980-. 6 issues per year. $239.00 (institutions). ISSN: 0143-4632.

This densely printed journal offers an international selection of research articles addressing ethnicity and language, language transfer, multiculturalism, multilingualism, and related topics. Book reviews in relevant areas are included. Also available electronically. Indexed in: *Current Index to Journals in Education, Linguistics and Language Behavior Abstracts, Multicultural Education Abstracts, Social Sciences Citation Index.*

261. **Journal of Negro Education.** Vol. 1-. Washington, D.C.: Howard University, 1932-. quarterly. $20.00 (institutions). ISSN: 0022-2984.

This highly regarded publication addresses all aspects of the education of African-American individuals in all types of educational settings and levels. Ranging from historical studies to current practices to innovative programs, the contents provide a forum for research and practice articles, and as the cover states, a "Review of Issues Incident to the Education of Black People." Includes book and media reviews. Indexed in: *Current Index to Journals in Education, Education Index, Higher Education Abstracts, Multicultural Education Abstracts, Psychological Abstracts, Sociology of Education Abstracts.*

262. **Language Learning: A Journal of Research in Language Studies.** Vol. 1-. Oxford, Eng.: Blackwell, 1948-. quarterly. $121.00 (institutions). ISSN: 0023-8333.

Research-based articles that deal with language learning, language acquisition, second language education, bilingualism, and literacy are included in this multidisciplinary journal. Research methods from many disciplines are represented. Indexed in: *Current Index to Journals in Education, Education Index, Linguistics and Language Behavior Abstracts, Multicultural Education Abstracts, Social Sciences Citation Index.*

263. **Multicultural Education**. Vol. 1-. San Francisco: Caddo Gap Press, 1993-. quarterly. $60.00 (institutions). ISSN: 1068-3844.

All levels of education are included in this journal devoted to multicultural education. Research articles, essays, opinion pieces, book and media reviews, reports of effective practices, and information about upcoming multicultural conferences and programs are regular features. Indexed in: *Current Index to Journals in Education, Sociology of Education Abstracts.*

264. **Race Ethnicity and Education**. Vol. 1-. Abingdon, Oxfordshire, Eng.: Carfax, 1998-. 2 issues per year. $135.00 (institutions). ISSN: 1361-3324.

This new internationally focused journal provides a forum for original research that explores the dynamics of race and ethnicity in educational theory, policy, and practice. As an interdisciplinary journal it draws from several social science disciplines and their respective methodologies. Indexed in: *Multicultural Education Abstracts, Sociology of Education Abstracts.*

265. **Teaching Tolerance**. Vol. 1-. Montgomery, Ala.: Southern Poverty Law Center, 1991-. 2 issues per year. free to educators. ISSN: 1066-2847.

Distributed semi-annually to educators free of charge, this frankly multicultural journal promotes tolerance and peace with classroom activities, teaching tips, inspirational stories, reviews of teaching resources, essays, and articles on practice. Multiculturalism in all of its aspects (special needs, cultural heritage, sexual orientation, gender) is addressed in this valuable classroom resource. Indexed in: *Current Index to Journals in Education.*

266. **TESOL Journal**. Vol. 1-. Alexandria, Va.: Teachers of English to Speakers of Other Languages, 1991-. quarterly. $58.00 (institutions). ISSN: 1056-7941.

A practical focus is the emphasis of research articles in this journal that addresses teaching English as a second, foreign, or additional language. All educational levels and settings are included. Topics covered include bilingual education, curriculum design, and teaching methodologies. Also includes book reviews, teaching tips, and an occasional thematic issue. Indexed in: *Current Index to Journals in Education.*

267. **TESOL Quarterly**. Vol. 1-. Alexandria, Va.: Teachers of English to Speakers of Other Languages, 1967-. quarterly. Subscription requires membership with additional charge for publications. ISSN: 0039-8322.

Listed as "A journal for teachers of English to speakers of other languages and of standard English as a second dialect," the sponsoring organization describes its mission as developing teaching expertise, fostering effective communication, and respecting diversity and individual language rights. The journal does this through articles that deal with both research and practice, regular reports of projects within the field, a forum for responding to published research, and book reviews that include classroom ESL texts. Indexed in: *Current Index to Journals in Education, Education Index, Linguistics and Language Behavior Abstracts, Multicultural Education Abstracts, Social Sciences Citation Index, Social Sciences Index.*

6

SPECIAL EDUCATION

Dictionaries and Encyclopedias

268. Accardo, Pasquale J., and Whitman, Barbara Y. **Dictionary of Developmental Disabilities Terminology**. Baltimore, Md.: Paul H. Brookes, 1996. 348 p. $55.00. LC: 95-47373. ISBN: 1-55766-112-X.

 This transdisciplinary dictionary includes developmental disabilities terminology from the fields of education, medicine, psychiatry, psychology, social work, family therapy, law, speech/language pathology, and physical therapy, among others. Selection of over 3,000 terms for inclusion was based on the likelihood of their use in an evaluation of a person with a developmental disability and that the reader of such reports would not necessarily be familiar with terms from other disciplines. Entries are clear and easy to understand, and where appropriate, include clarifying illustrations. Useful in a variety of settings.

269. Reynolds, Cecil R., and Mann, Lester, ed. **Encyclopedia of Special Education: A Reference for the Education of the Handicapped and Other Exceptional Children and Adults**. New York: John Wiley & Sons, 1987. 3 vol. $525.00. LC: 86-33975. ISBN: 0471-82858-0.

 Although somewhat dated, this encyclopedia still offers authoritative information on key topics in special education. Arranged alphabetically, entries include descriptions of tests and assessments, biographies of pivotal individuals, intervention techniques and services, descriptions of specific disabilities, legal and legislative issues, and a variety of other topics related to special education. Each entry includes bibliographic references and cross-references to other relevant topics within the encyclopedia. The text of Public Law 94-142 is appended. Indexes to names and subjects are also provided.

270.   Vergason, Glenn A., and Anderegg, M. L., ed. **Dictionary of Special Education and Rehabilitation**. 4th ed. Denver, Colo.: Love Publishing, 1997. 210 p. $32.00. LC: 95-82151. ISBN: 0-89108-243-3. First published as the *Dictionary of Exceptional Children*, 1971.

Not only an excellent source of information for special education and rehabilitation terminology, this directory offers separate listings of key organizations in the field, abbreviations and acronyms, periodicals and journals, legal terms, and sources of legal assistance. Compiled from terms used in texts and professional books, the terms reflect current use and practice within special education and rehabilitation.

271.   Williams, Phillip. **The Special Education Handbook: An Introductory Reference**. Buckingham, Eng.: Open University Press, 1991. 434 p. $150.00. LC: 90-35680. ISBN: 0-335-09314-0.

Designed as a dictionary rather than a handbook, Williams' work provides over 1,000 terms that are important to the field of special education. Although the focus is on special education within Great Britain, terms that are used internationally, particularly from North America, and that appear in published literature, are included. Due to the extensive inclusion of research and testing terminology, the definitions are useful regardless of geographic locale.

Directories and Almanacs

272.   **Complete Learning Disabilities Directory, 1998/99**. 6th ed. Lakeville, Conn.: Grey House Publishing, 1998. 642 p. $145.00. ISBN: 0-939300-07-0.

Included in this directory are schools, learning centers, vocational training programs, camps, associations and organizations, government agencies, testing, print and nonprint resources, and relevant conferences and workshops related to learning disabilities. Very brief data is provided for each entry, generally only address and telephone and FAX numbers. Some entries include brief descriptive sentences. Thorough indexing is provided.

273. **Directory for Exceptional Children: A Listing of Educational and Training Facilities 1994-95**. 13th ed. Boston: Porter Sargent Publishers, 1994. 1,310 p. $80.00. LC: 54-4975. ISBN: 0-87558-131-5.

Prefaced with illustrated advertising for programs and facilities for exceptional children, the directory segment of this work lists fifteen categories of services with brief standardized descriptions. Included are schools and clinics for the learning disabled, psychiatric and guidance clinics, schools for the blind and partially sighted, and speech and hearing clinics. Each entry includes information regarding whether the facility is coeducational, residential or day school; ages served, enrollment, staff; costs; contact information; type of treatment; and a brief description. Also listed are associations and federal and state agencies that provide services and information for exceptional children and their families. An index by facility name is included. Useful directory to services, programs and facilities for special populations.

274. **Directory of College Facilities and Services for People with Disabilities**. 4th ed. Phoenix, Ariz.: Oryx Press, 1996. 423 p. $125.00. ISSN: 1085-9411. ISBN: 0-89774-894-8.

Extremely valuable guide to colleges and universities providing services and facilities for people with disabilities. A listing of U.S. and Canadian colleges provides basic information about the institution, campus accessibility and special facilities, and special services. Enrollment figures include the general population as well as numbers of students with disabilities and the type of disability. Useful resource for college applicants, counselors, and rehabilitation professionals.

Guides, Handbooks, and Yearbooks

275. Buchanan, Mary, Weller, Carol, and Buchanan, Michelle. **Special Education Desk Reference**. San Diego: Singular Publishing Group, 1997. 314 p. $55.00. ISBN: 1-56593-800-3.

Offers practical guidance to those working with the gifted or persons with disabilities. The focus is on methods, techniques, and interventions used with special populations. In addition to describing each method, source documentation is provided, as are any qualifying notes. Addresses early childhood; giftedness; language, reading, mathematics, computer, seminal, written expression and transition methods; physical education, and other specific needs. Valuable guide for the practitioner.

276.   Colangelo, Nicholas, and Davis, Gary A., ed. **Handbook of Gifted Education**. 2nd ed. Boston: Allyn and Bacon, 1997. 582 p. $70.00. LC: 96-19246. ISBN: 0-205-26085-3.

Useful as both a handbook on gifted education and as a textbook for college courses. This resource, divided into six sections, provides an overview and history of gifted education; identification of giftedness; teaching practices and models; creativity and thinking skills; counseling services; and, special topics/special populations. Authors of the 44 chapters are well-known in the field of gifted education.

277.   Compton, Carolyn. **A Guide to 100 Tests for Special Education**. New ed. Upper Saddle, N.J.: Globe Fearon, 1996. 346 p. ISBN: 0-8359-1611-1.

Designed to inform teachers about specific tests, this guide profiles 100 tests used to assess academic strengths or deficiencies. Each test is described with additional information about its strengths and limiting factors. The introduction provides background information to testing, its uses and misuses, and interpreting results and communicating with parents. Helpful guide to instruments used to assess learning difficulties and related problems.

278.   Council for Exceptional Children. **What Every Special Educator Must Know: The International Standards for the Preparation and Certification of Special Education Teachers**. Reston, Va.: Council for Exceptional Children, 1995. 139 p. $14.30. LC: 95-39777. ISBN: 0-86586-274-5.

Valuable compendium of the standards and guidelines for preparation and certification of special educators. Included are the code of ethics and standards of professional practice for special educators, as well as standards and guidelines for teachers working with students with specific exceptionalities. An overview of the standards, their development, and application helps to put this material into context. Despite the lack of an index, the table of contents provides adequate access to the standards and their content.

279.   **Educational Opportunity Guide: A Directory of Programs for the Gifted**. Durham, N.C.: Duke University Talent Identification Program, 1998. 338 p. $15.00. ISBN: 0-9639756-4-1.

Annual guide to programs for the gifted provides information about programs at schools, colleges, and camps in the U.S. and abroad. Although programs are included for elementary through secondary school students, the emphasis is on the latter. Programs are listed by state, and indexes provide access by grade level, gender, format, and topic. Other sections provide information about international programs, resources for the gifted, academic competitions, and paid advertising for specific programs.

280. Heller, Kurt A., Monks, Franz J., and Passow, A. Harry, ed. **International Handbook of Research and Development of Giftedness and Talent**. Oxford, Eng.: Pergamon Press, 1993. 964 p. $231.00. LC: 93-16813. ISBN: 0-08-041398-6.

Incorporating 80 contributors from 18 countries, this handbook strives to present an international focus on giftedness and talent. Divided into seven sections, the 53 chapters address historical and ongoing issues, conceptions and development, identification, programs and practices, nurturing giftedness and talent, examples of international programs and policies, and, present and future directions. Extensive references at the end of each chapter provide solid documentation of past and current research. The subject index is particularly valuable in locating specific topics within the chapters.

281. Wang, Margaret C., Reynolds, Maynard C., and Walberg, Herbert J. **Handbook of Special and Remedial Education: Research and Practice**. 2nd ed. Oxford, Eng.: Pergamon, 1995. 468 p. $165.00. LC: 95-37011. ISBN: 0-08-042566-6.

The first edition was published between 1987-1991 in four volumes as the *Handbook of Special Education*. This second edition, with fifteen chapters, offers a research-based guide and overview of intervention and practice in special and remedial education. The volume is comprised of three sections: Learners at the Margins; Distinct Disabilities; and Support Systems. Each chapter is written by authorities in their respective fields and includes extensive references.

Indexes and Abstracts

282. **Exceptional Child Education Resources**. Reston, Va.: Council for Exceptional Children, 1969-. v. 30, 1998. $89.00 (nonmembers); $69.00 (CEC members). ISSN: 0160-4309.

Quarterly abstracting tool that covers books, journal articles, and other print and nonprint media related to disabilities, giftedness, and other topics in special education. The populations covered range from infants to older adults. Affiliated with the ERIC system, there is extensive overlap between materials indexed in ECER and ERIC. Author, title, and subject indexes supplement the abstracted material as does a list of over 200 source journals from which articles are selected for review. Sufficient unique material is abstracted to justify purchase of this title, even when the ERIC system is available. Also available electronically.

283. **Special Educational Needs Abstracts**. Vol. 1-. Abingdon, Oxfordshire, Eng.: Carfax, 1989-. quarterly-. $472.00 (institutions). ISSN: 0954-0822.

Provides references and non-evaluative abstracts to British special education literature, including journal articles, books, and other reports. Special needs addressed include physical, intellectual, emotional, or social problems. Subject and author indexes appear in each issue and a cumulative author and subject issue is provided at the end of each volume.

Journals

284. **Behavioral Disorders**. Vol. 1-. Reston, Va.: Council for Children with Behavioral Disorders, 1976-. quarterly. $50.00 (institutions). ISSN: 0198-7249.

Focusing on the education of students with emotional and behavioral disorders, this journal publishes research reports, program evaluations, and position papers, with a strong emphasis given to intervention and assessment. Indexed in: *Current Index to Journals in Education, Education Index, Exceptional Child Education Resources.*

285. **British Journal of Special Education**. Vol. 1-. Oxford, Eng.: Blackwell, 1974-. quarterly. $156.00 (nonmembers). ISSN: 0952-3383.

Sponsored by the National Association for Special Needs, this British publication includes research articles, association information, updates on current mandates, and book reviews. Articles are of general interest to those in special education; some material may only be of interest to those studying or involved in British special education practices and research. Indexed in: *British Education Index, Current Index to Journals in Education, Exceptional Child Education Abstracts, Sociology of Education Abstracts, Special Educational Needs Abstracts.*

286. **Career Development for Exceptional Individuals**. Vol. 1- . Reston, Va.: Division on Career Development and Transition, Council for Exceptional Children, 1978-. 2 issues per year. $20.00 (institutions). ISSN: 0885-7288.

Another quality publication from the Council for Exceptional Children, this twice yearly journal offers research-based articles addressing the transition from school to work for exceptional individuals. Book reviews of relevant materials are also included. Indexed in: *Current Index to Journals in Education, Exceptional Child Education Resources.*

287. **Education and Training in Mental Retardation and Developmental Disabilities**. Vol. 1-. Reston, Va.: Division on Mental Retardation and Developmental Disabilities, Council for Exceptional Children, 1966-. quarterly. $75.00 (institutions). ISSN: 0013-1237.

Focuses on identification and assessment, educational programming, characteristics, teacher training, prevention, community interactions, and legislation as they affect the education and welfare of persons with mental retardation and developmental disabilities. Articles are refereed, with research, practice, and literature reviews predominating. Indexed in: *Current Index to Journals in Education, Educational Administration Abstracts, Exceptional Child Education Resources, Linguistics and Language Behavior Abstracts, Psychological Abstracts, Social Sciences Citation Index, Special Educational Needs Abstracts.*

288. **Exceptional Children**. Vol. 1-. Reston, Va.: Council for Exceptional Children, 1934-. quarterly. $58.00 (institutions). ISSN: 0014-4029.

Publishing original research on the education and development of exceptional children, this official publication of the Council for Exceptional Children also provides association news, job advertisements, and articles of professional interest to special educators. Included are articles about individuals from infancy through adolescence with disabilities or giftedness. Indexed in: *Current Index to Journals in Education, Education Index, Exceptional Child Education Resources, Multicultural Education Abstracts, Psychological Abstracts, Social Sciences Citation Index, Special Educational Needs Abstracts, Sociology of Education Abstracts.*

289. **Exceptionality**. Vol. 1- . Mahwah, N.J.: Lawrence Erlbaum, 1990-. quarterly. $175.00 (institutions). ISSN: 0936-2835.

The official journal of the Division for Research of the Council for Exceptional Children focuses on original research and research reviews related to individuals with disabilities or giftedness. Applied research on exceptional individuals of any age are included. Indexed in: *Current Index to Journals in Education, Exceptional Child Education Resources, Psychological Abstracts.*

290.   **Gifted Child Quarterly**. Vol. 1-. Washington, D.C.: National Association for Gifted Children, 1957-. quarterly. $50.00 (institutions). ISSN: 0016-9862.

Research articles and book reviews on gifted and talented children and their identification, education, and nurturing comprise the contents of this association-sponsored journal. Special thematic issues are periodically published. Indexed in: *Current Index to Journals in Education, Education Index, Exceptional Child Education Resources, Psychological Abstracts, Social Sciences Citation Index.*

291.   **Gifted Education International**. Vol. 1-. Bicester, Oxon, Eng.: A B Academic Publishers, 1982-. 3 issues per year. $99.00. ISSN: 0261-4294.

With its strong international focus, this journal provides a forum for practical and research articles on provisions for the education and support of gifted and talented individuals. Book reviews, reports of successful programs, and contributions from gifted students are included. Indexed in: *Current Index to Journals in Education, Exceptional Child Education Resources, Psychological Abstracts.*

292.   **International Journal of Disability, Development and Education**. Vol. 1-. Abingdon, Oxfordshire, Eng.: Carfax, 1954-. quarterly. $248.00 (institutions). ISSN: 1034-912X.

Formerly *Exceptional Child* and *Slow Learning Child*. Brief reports and theory, research, and practice articles dealing with disability, human development, and education are presented. International in coverage, cross-cultural studies as well as research on special education and rehabilitation in developed and developing countries are included. Indexed in: *Current Index to Journals in Education, Education Index, Exceptional Child Education Resources, Multicultural Education Abstracts, Psychological Abstracts, Social Sciences Citation Index, Sociology of Education Abstracts.*

293.   **Intervention in School and Clinic**. Vol. 1-. Austin, Tex.: PRO-ED, 1965-. 5 issues per year. $95.00 (institutions). ISSN: 1053-4512.

Formerly *Academic Therapy*. Practical methods and techniques for working with special needs individuals, book and product reviews, research articles, and teaching tips are presented in this useful publication directed to educators, clinicians, parents and therapists. Remedial as well as special education issues are addressed. Also available electronically. Indexed in: *Current Index to Journals in Education, Education Index, Exceptional Child Education*

Resources, Psychological Abstracts, Social Sciences Citation Index, Special Educational Needs Abstracts.

294. **Journal for the Education of the Gifted**. Vol. 1-. Waco, Tex.: Prufrock Press, 1977-. quarterly. $48.00 (institutions). ISSN: 0162-3532.

As the official journal of the Association for the Gifted, a division of the Council for Exceptional Children, an array of theoretical, descriptive, and research articles are presented in each volume. Essays and opinion pieces representing diverse points of view regarding the education of the gifted and talented are included as are literature reviews and historical overviews. Indexed in: *Current Index to Journals in Education, Educational Administration Abstracts, Exceptional Child Education Resources, Multicultural Education Abstracts, Psychological Abstracts, and Social Sciences Citation Index.*

295. **Journal of Developmental Education**. Vol. 1-. Boone, N.C.: National Center for Developmental Education, Appalachian State University, 1978-. 3 issues per year. $32.00 (institutions). ISSN: 0894-3907.

The official journal of the National Center for Developmental Education provides association news, opinion columns, brief reports, and research articles on developmental and remedial education. College level remediation and development of basic education skills are the focus of this publication. Formerly *Journal of Developmental and Remedial Education*. Indexed in: *Current Index to Journals in Education, Education Index, Higher Education Abstracts, Multicultural Education Abstracts.*

296. **Journal of Early Intervention** . Vol. 1-. Reston, Va.: Division for Early Childhood, Council for Exceptional Children, 1979-. quarterly. $70.00. ISSN: 1053-8151.

Formerly *Journal of the Division for Early Childhood*, the focus of this publication is on early intervention for infants and young children with special needs or at risk for developmental disabilities. Research and practice articles, reports of replicable innovative programs and techniques, policy analyses, and research method articles are included. Emphasis is placed on minority, culturally different, and international children. Indexed in: *Current Index to Journals in Education, Exceptional Child Education Resources, Multicultural Education Abstracts, Psychological Abstracts, Social Sciences Citation Index.*

297. **Journal of Education for Students Placed at Risk**. Vol. 1-. Mahwah, N.J.: Lawrence Erlbaum, 1996-. quarterly. $135.00 (institutions). ISSN: 1082-4669.

   Emphasis is given to practical research-based information for educators, academic researchers, and policy analysts involved in the education of students at risk. Regular updates on Title I are included as are book reviews, case studies, program descriptions, and research articles. Indexed in: *Current Index to Journals in Education, Exceptional Child Education Resources, Sociology of Education Abstracts.*

298. **Journal of Learning Disabilities**. Vol. 1-. Austin, Tex.: PRO-ED, 1968-. 6 issues per year. $120.00 (institutions). ISSN: 0022-2194.

   Research articles, theoretical papers, intervention articles, position papers, literature reviews, and practice reports related to learning disabilities at all educational levels are included in this journal. Indexed in: *Current Index to Journals in Education, Education Index, Educational Administration Abstracts, Exceptional Child Education Resources, Higher Education Abstracts, Multicultural Education Abstracts, Psychological Abstracts, Social Sciences Citation Index, Special Educational Needs Abstracts.*

299. **Journal of Special Education**. Vol. 1-. Austin, Tex.: PRO-ED, 1966-. quarterly. $95.00 (institutions). ISSN: 0022-4669.

   Research, essay, and commentary articles pertaining to the education of individuals with special needs appear in this publication. Articles address a wide array of concerns including numbers of minority students in special education, gifted education, and specific interventions. Also available electronically. Indexed in: *Current Index to Journals in Education, Education Index, Exceptional Child Education Resources, Psychological Abstracts, Social Sciences Citation Index, Special Educational Needs Abstracts.*

300. **Journal of the Association for Persons with Severe Handicaps**. Vol. 1-. Baltimore, Md.: Association for Persons with Severe Handicaps, 1975-. quarterly. $190.00 (institutions). ISSN: 0274-9483.

   As the official publication of the Association, this journal provides intervention strategies, assessment methodologies for special populations, reviews, program and practice descriptions, and research articles. Also available electronically. Former title *AAESPH Review.* Indexed in: *Current Index to Journals in Education, Education Index, Exceptional Child Education Resources, Psychological Abstracts, Social Sciences Citation Index.*

301. **Learning Disability Quarterly** . Vol. 1-. Overland, Kans.: Council for Learning Disabilities, 1978-. quarterly. $55.00 (institutions). ISSN: 0731-9487.

As the journal of the Council for Learning Disabilities, the focus is on educational articles with an applied aspect. Research and theoretical articles, literature reviews, reports of methodology, legislative information, and descriptions of professional training programs are included. Indexed in: *Current Index to Journals in Education, Education Index, Exceptional Child Education Resources, Multicultural Education Abstracts, Psychological Abstracts, Social Sciences Citation Index, Special Educational Needs Abstracts.*

302. **Mental Retardation**. Vol. 1-. Washington, D.C.: American Association on Mental Retardation (AAMR), 1963-. bimonthly. $115.00. ISSN: 0047-6765.

Association news, book reviews, essays, program descriptions, policy analyses, and research articles appear in AAMR's bimonthly publication. Articles with an applied focus on mental retardation research are featured, and the context is often within an educational setting. Indexed in: *Current Index to Journals in Education, Education Index, Exceptional Child Education Resources, Multicultural Education Abstracts, Psychological Abstracts, Social Sciences Citation Index, Sociology of Education Abstracts, Special Educational Needs Abstracts.*

303. **RE:view: Rehabilitation and Education for Blindness and Visual Impairment**. Vol. 1-. Washington, D.C.: Heldref, 1951-. quarterly. $62.00 (institutions). ISSN: 0899-1510.

Published for the Association for Education and Rehabilitation of the Blind and Visually Impaired, this journal provides relevant reports of practice, research articles, and teaching tips. Indexed in: *Current Index to Journals in Education, Education Index, Educational Administration Abstracts, Exceptional Child Education Resources, Psychological Abstracts, Special Educational Needs Abstracts.*

304. **Remedial and Special Education**. Vol.1-. Austin, Tex.: PRO-ED, 1984-. bimonthly. $110.00 (institutions). ISSN: 0741-9325.

Emphasizing research articles with practical applications, *RASE* includes information useful to the practitioner, administrator, teacher educator, and teacher-in-training working in remedial and special education. Book reviews, a calendar of upcoming conferences, and classified advertising are included. Indexed in: *Current*

Index to Journals in Education, Education Index, Exceptional Child Education Resources, Multicultural Education Abstracts, Psychological Abstracts, Social Sciences Citation Index, Special Educational Needs Abstracts.

305.   **Roeper Review: A Journal on Gifted Education**. Vol. 1-. Bloomfield Hills, Mich.: Roeper School, 1979-. quarterly. $73.00 (institutions). ISSN: 0278-3193.

Gifted and talented education are explored through research, theory and practice articles, observation studies, program reports, and book reviews. Issues related to the gifted and talented across the lifespan are included. Also available electronically. Indexed in: *Current Index to Journals in Education, Education Index, Exceptional Child Education Resources, Psychological Abstracts.*

306.   **Teacher Education and Special Education**. Vol. 1-. Albany, N.Y.: Boyd Printing Co., 1977-. quarterly. $62.00 (institutions). ISSN: 0888-4064.

The official journal of the Teacher Education Division of the Council for Exceptional Children provides a forum for research related to the preparation of teachers working with exceptional and special needs students. Research articles, program descriptions, and book reviews are included. Indexed in: *Current Index to Journals in Education, Education Index, Exceptional Child Education Resources.*

307.   **Teaching Exceptional Children** . Vol. 1-. Reston, Va.: Council for Exceptional Children (CEC), 1968-. 6 issues per year. $58.00 (institutions). ISSN: 0040-0599.

Association information, reviews of relevant ERIC items, and practical methods and materials for working with children with disabilities or who are gifted are presented in this CEC official publication. Valuable resource for the practitioner working with exceptional children. Indexed in: *Current Index to Journals in Education, Education Index, Exceptional Child Education Resources.*

308.   **Topics in Early Childhood Special Education**. Vol. 1-. Austin, Tex.: PRO-ED, 1981-. quarterly. $95.00 (institutions). ISSN: 0271-1214.

Directed to those working with young children with special needs, this quarterly publication offers research and practice articles on topics such as assessment, intervention, public policy, and adaptive and assistive technologies. Thematic issues are published periodically. Also available electronically. Indexed in: *Current Index to Journals in Education, Education Index, Exceptional Child Education Resources, Multicultural Education Abstracts, Psychological Abstracts, Social Sciences Citation Index, Special Educational Needs Abstracts.*

7

ADULT, ALTERNATIVE, CONTINUING, AND DISTANCE EDUCATION

Dictionaries and Encyclopedias

309. Jarvis, Peter. **An International Dictionary of Adult and Continuing Education**. New York: Routledge, 1990. 372 p. $69.95. LC: 89-33895. ISBN: 0-415-02421-8.

One of the strengths of this specialized dictionary is its international focus. Terms, names of associations, awards, programs, and publications are included from all over the world. Many general education terms are included as well. As the author acknowledges in his preface, with the rapid change in technology and information, many of the terms will be outdated almost immediately upon publication. The technological advances in distance education alone would reinforce that. Nonetheless, the extensive inclusion of terms related to international adult and continuing education make this a most useful tool.

310. Tuijnman, Albert C., ed. **International Encyclopedia of Adult Education and Training**. 2nd ed. Oxford, Eng.: Pergamon, 1996. 960 p. (*Resources in Education [Pergamon]*). $203.75. LC: 95-53922. ISBN: 0-08-042305-1.

Drawing from articles in the second edition of the *International Encyclopedia of Education*, this work contains 161 revised or new articles that address issues of lifelong learning and adult and continuing education in an international context. Sections focus on concepts, theories and methods; policies, costs and finance; human development and adult learning; educational technology; participation and provision; organization; and evaluation and measurement. An extensive subject index provides detailed information about the contents of each article, while a thorough author index provides access to the many authors cited in each article as well as to the contributing authors. Further reading suggestions are also provided at the end of each article. More of a handbook than an encyclopedia, this compilation of articles provides a wealth of information about adult education.

Directories and Almanacs

311. Burgess, William E. **Oryx Guide to Distance Learning: A Comprehensive Listing of Electronic and Other Media-Assisted Courses**. 2nd ed. Phoenix, Ariz.: Oryx Press, 1997. 497 p. $116.50. LC: 97-8597. ISBN: 1-57356-073-1.

Over 1,400 media-assisted courses at 434 institutions are described in this directory. Organized by state and institution, each entry includes contact information, delivery systems, institution description (accreditation, admission requirements, costs, facilities, grading, and degree credit), and courses offered. Delivery systems range from audiocassettes to the Internet. Indexes provide access by subject, type of delivery system, and name of institution. Listings of consortially delivered courses are also included. Useful guide to a rapidly expanding area of education.

312. **Independent Study Catalog**. 7th ed. Washington, D.C.: Peterson's for the University Continuing Education Association, 1998. 388 p. $21.95. ISBN: 0-768900-08-5.

Focusing primarily on correspondence courses, but including those using multiple forms of delivery services beyond mail, this directory lists schools and institutions that provide accredited courses of study from elementary through higher education levels. Each institution is listed with contact information, eligibility requirements, and a list of courses offered. Most courses are at the college level but others are included as well. Introductory pages address financial issues, mechanics of distance learning, and eligibility concerns. Indexes provide access by location of programs and by subject areas. Helpful guide to correspondence study and distance learning.

313. **Peterson's Distance Learning 1997**. Princeton, N.J.: Peterson's, 1996. 486 p. $24.95. ISBN: 1-56079-664-2.

Distance education programs at more than 750 institutions are listed in this directory. Programs are geared for college and university students and are accredited. Arranged alphabetically by institution name, each description includes general information, accessibility, delivery systems, facilities, application procedures, costs, and contact information. A separate section includes lengthier promotional descriptions written by the institutions. Indexes provide access by degree and certificate programs, individual course offerings, geographic location, and participation in public broadcasting telecourses. Presents a solid source of information on distance education programs.

314. Sullivan, Eugene. **The Adult Learner's Guide to Alternative and External Degree Programs**. Phoenix, Ariz.: Oryx Press, 1993. 227 p. (*American Council on Education Series on Higher Education*). $39.95. LC: 93-32154. ISBN: 0-89774-815-8.

Based on a survey conducted by the American Council of Education, this guide lists degree programs for adult learners. The alternative degree programs include those with schedules designed to meet adult needs and are usually campus based. The external degree programs are those with less than 25 percent of the degree requirements based on campus, and generally incorporate distance education. In addition to state-by-state listings of both types of accredited degree programs, the appendixes include guidelines for quality programs and indexes to institutions and fields of study.

Guides, Handbooks, and Yearbooks

315. Mintz, Jerry, Solomon, Raymond, and Solomon, Sidney, ed. **Handbook of Alternative Education**. New York: Macmillan, 1994. 431 p. $153.00. LC: 94-13903. ISBN: 0-02-897303-8.

With nearly 7,500 entries, alternative education options at all levels of education are presented. However, the majority fall within the elementary and secondary education areas. Included are Montessori, Waldorf, Quaker, charter schools, and home-based programs. The handbook includes an introduction, a section of viewpoints on different forms of alternative education, vignettes from different alternative programs, a bibliography, listings by type of school, and an index by name of school or program. The majority of the work is devoted to state listings of alternative programs arranged in zip code order. Each entry includes contact information, type of school and affiliations, enrollment, staffing, costs, accreditation, governance, teacher qualifications, and special features. Helpful resource for identifying alternative education options.

316. Thorson, Marcie Kisner. **Campus-Free College Degrees**. 8th ed. Tulsa, Okla.: Thorson Guides, 1998. 304 p. $24.95. ISSN: 1043-2086. ISBN: 0-916277-48-8.

This guide to obtaining a college degree without on-campus class attendance is geared to the increasing interest in distance education. Brief introductions about distance learning, accreditation, equivalency exams, and obtaining high school diplomas are followed by an alphabetical listing of institutions with accredited distance degree programs. Each entry includes contact information, a description of the program, costs, and requirements. Indexes by areas of study, schools by state and by school name enhance access points.

World Wide Web and Internet Sources

317. **World Lecture Hall**. http://www.utexas.edu/world/lecture/index.html (accessed February 28, 1999).

Particularly valuable for distance education programs, this site provides course syllabi, lecture notes, class calendars, and assignments for courses taught through the Internet or that supply materials via the Internet. A search feature is included as well as lists of subject areas with links to resources. Also included are links to home pages for U.S. universities and community colleges.

Journals

318. **Adult Education Quarterly: A Journal of Research and Theory in Adult Education**. Vol. 1-. Washington, D.C.: American Association for Adult and Continuing Education, 1950-. quarterly. $39.00 (institutions). ISSN: 0741-7136.

Formerly *Adult Education*. Focusing on research and theory in adult and continuing education, the journal also includes literature reviews, critiques and responses to previously published articles, and book reviews. Indexed in: *Current Index to Journals in Education, Education Index, Sociology of Education Abstracts, Social Sciences Citation Index*.

319. **Adult Learning**. Vol. 1-. Washington, D.C.: American Association for Adult and Continuing Education, 1990-. quarterly. $29.00 (institutions). ISSN: 1045-1595.

AACE provides a forum for practical articles, recent trends, and new resources in this quarterly publication. Research articles appear in AACE's *Adult Education Quarterly*. Indexed in: *Current Index to Journals in Education, Education Index*.

320. **American Journal of Distance Education**. Vol. 1-. University Park, Pa.: American Center for the Study of Distance Education, Pennsylvania State University, 1987-. quarterly. $65.00 (institutions). ISSN: 0892-3647.

Through research and practical articles this journal addresses all types of media and communication in the role of distance education in various milieus (military, industry, and elementary through higher education). Includes book reviews. Indexed in: *Current Index to Journals in Education, Higher Education Abstracts, Research into Higher Education*.

321. **Convergence**. Vol. 1-. Toronto, Ont., Canada: International Council for Adult Education, 1968-. quarterly. $39.00. ISSN: 0010-8146.

This international journal addresses issues, practice, and research in adult and nonformal education. Book reviews are also included. Indexed in: *Current Index to Journals in Education*.

322. **Journal of Continuing Higher Education**. Vol. 1-. Charleston, S.C.: Trident Technical College, attn. Wayne Whelan, 1952-. 3 issues per year. $40.00. ISSN: 0737-7363.

As the journal of the Association for Continuing Higher Education, the contents address research, observations, and practical reports related to continuing higher education. Book reviews and association news and reports are regularly featured. Distance education, adult and nontraditional students, and innovative practices are among the topics covered. Indexed in: *Current Index to Journals in Education*.

323. **New Directions for Adult and Continuing Education**. Vol. 1-. San Francisco: Jossey-Bass, 1979-. quarterly. (*Jossey-Bass Higher and Adult Education Series*). $99.00 (institutions). ISSN: 1052-2891.

Research and practice articles on adult and continuing education are issued in quarterly thematic issues, each with its own monographic title. Collaborative learning, the Internet, literacy programs, and experiential learning are examples of recent thematic issues. Valuable resource for background information and recent research on specific topics. Indexed in: *Current Index to Journals in Education, Education Index, Higher Education Abstracts, Multicultural Education Abstracts*.

324.   **Open Learning**. Vol. 1-. London: Pitman Publishing, 1974-. 3 issues per year. $120.00. ISSN: 0268-0513.

Sponsored by the Open University, the focus of this journal is on open learning and distance education primarily in United Kingdom institutions of higher education. Distance education at the international level is also addressed. Research articles, opinion pieces, book reviews, conference reports, and program descriptions are included. Indexed in: *Current Index to Journals in Education, Higher Education Abstracts, Research into Higher Education Abstracts, Sociology of Education Abstracts.*

8

CAREER AND
VOCATIONAL EDUCATION

Directories and Almanacs

325. Wright, Philip C., Guidry, Josee G., and Blair, Judy. **Opportunities for Vocational Study: A Directory of Learning Programs Sponsored by North American Non-Profit Associations**. Toronto, Ont., Canada: University of Toronto Press, 1994. 412 p. ISBN: 0-8020-7776-5.

Excellent source of information about vocational training and certification in Canada and the United States. The directory provides information of interest to those seeking vocational and further career training and to career counselors. The focus is on business and industry with some inclusion of technical training programs. The allied health fields are generally not included, unless the focus is on management. Each entry provides basic address information, a description of training programs, the form of instructional delivery, admission requirements, if any, and recertification procedures.

Guides, Handbooks, and Yearbooks

326. **Educators Guide to Free Guidance Materials**. 36th ed. Randolph, Wis.: Educators Progress Service, 1997. 256 p. $28.95. LC: 62-18761.

Divided into listings for different media formats and print guidance materials, this guide offers materials in four categories: career planning, social/personal, responsibility to self and others, and use of leisure time. Title, source, and subject indexes provide additional access points. Although all items listed are free, some materials are twenty years old, while others are very current. Sources include businesses, organizations, government agencies, religious groups, and others.

Journals

327.   **British Journal of Guidance and Counselling** . Vol. 1-. Abingdon, Oxfordshire, Eng.: Carfax, 1973-. quarterly. $308.00. ISSN: 0306-9885.

Articles addressing both theoretical and practical issues within the field of guidance and counseling are included in this British publication. Book reviews, case studies, and brief reports are also provided. Of interest to counselors, educators, researchers, psychotherapists, and social workers. Indexed in: *British Education Index, Current Index to Journals in Education, Psychological Abstracts, Research into Higher Education Abstracts, Sociology of Education Abstracts.*

328.   **Business Education Forum**. Vol.1-. Reston, Va.: National Business Education Association, 1946-. quarterly. $20.00 (membership). ISSN: 0007-6678.

The official publication of the National Business Education Association offers articles of interest to the practitioner as well as association information. Regularly addressed are curricular issues and classroom methodologies as well as ways to improve student learning. Indexed in: *Business Education Index, Current Index to Journals in Education.*

329.   **Career Development Quarterly**. Vol. 1-. Alexandria, Va.: National Career Development Association, 1952-. quarterly. $61.00 (institutions). ISSN: 0889-4019.

Includes articles about career education, career counseling, career development, and work and leisure, generally with a practical focus. Both research-based articles and monograph-length works may appear in each issue. Indexed in: *Current Index to Journals in Education, Education Index, Higher Education Abstracts, Social Sciences Citation Index.*

330.   **Counselor Education and Supervision**. Vol. 1-. Alexandria, Va.: American Counseling Association, 1962-. quarterly. $40.00. ISSN: 0011-0035.

Directed to the preparation and training of counselors at all levels of education and types of educational settings, this journal includes research, theory, and practice articles. Indexed in: *Current*

Index to Journals in Education, Education Index, Higher Education Abstracts, Psychological Abstracts, Social Sciences Citation Index.

331. **Journal of Agricultural Education**. Vol. 1-. Huntsville, Tex.: American Association for Agricultural Education, 1959-. quarterly. $95.00 (nonmembers). ISSN: 1042-0541.

Previously *Journal of the American Association of Teacher Educators in Agriculture*, this publication provides research-based international articles on agricultural education and extension. Indexed in: *Current Index to Journals in Education.*

332. **Journal of Career Development**. Vol. 1-. New York: Human Sciences Press, 1972-. quarterly. $265.00 (institutions). ISSN: 0894-8453.

Research, theory, and practice articles related to career development are the focus of this journal, with a strong emphasis on the impact of theory and research on practice. Career education; career and leisure; and career development for adults, special needs populations, and those with families are considered within this publication's framework. Indexed in: *Business Education Index, Current Index to Journals in Education, Higher Education Abstracts, Psychological Abstracts, Social Sciences Citation Index.*

333. **Journal of Cooperative Education**. Vol. 1-. Columbia, Md.: Cooperative Education Association, 1964-. 3 issues per year. $30.00 (institutions). ISSN: 0022-0132.

Program descriptions, essays, and research articles are presented in this journal devoted to work-integrated education. School-to-work programs, marketing, industry partnerships, and training are some of the topics addressed. Indexed in: *Current Index to Journals in Education, Education Index.*

334. **Journal of Industrial Teacher Education**. Vol. 1-. Murfreesboro, Tenn.: Middle Tennessee State University, Attn. James H. Lorenz, 1963-. quarterly. $30.00. ISSN: 0022-1864.

Published for the National Association of Industrial and Technical Teacher Educators, the contents focus on industrial and technical teacher education, military training, and industrial training. Includes book and media reviews, essays and commentaries, theme issues, and research articles. Indexed in: *Current Index to Journals in Education, Education Index.*

335. **Journal of Vocational Behavior**. Vol. 1-. Orlando, Fla.: Academic Press, 1971-. bimonthly. $525.00 (institutions). ISSN: 0001-8791.

Empirical, methodological, and theoretical articles addressing vocational choice and vocational adjustment among different
populations are featured in this journal. Topics include job satisfac-
tion, career choice, occupational stereotyping, and career patterns
and career development. Also available electronically. Indexed in:
*Current Index to Journals in Education, Higher Education Ab-
stracts, Psychological Abstracts, Social Sciences Citation Index.*

336.   **Journal of Vocational Education and Training**. Vol. 1-. Wallingford, Oxfordshire, Eng.: Triangle Journals, 1949-. quarterly.
$214.00 (institutions). ISSN: 1363-6820.

Formerly *The Vocational Aspect of Education*, this refereed
journal has an international focus. Articles focus on work-related
education in both its theory and practice. Pre-vocational as well as
vocational education is considered. Indexed in: *Current Index to
Journals in Education, Multicultural Education Abstracts, Research into Higher Education Abstracts, Sociology of Education
Abstracts.*

337.   **Journal of Vocational Education Research**. Vol. 1-. Athens, Ga.:
Department of Occupational Studies, University of Georgia, 1976-.
quarterly. $57.00 (nonmembers). ISSN: 0739-3369.

As an official publication of the American Vocational Educational Research Association, the focus is on vocational education,
preparation for work, and the workplace in research-based articles.
Empirical, conceptual, and philosophical articles; literature reviews; historical studies; book reviews; and commentaries are
included. Indexed in: *Current Index to Journals in Education,
Education Index.*

9

COMPARATIVE AND
INTERNATIONAL EDUCATION

Dictionaries and Encyclopedias

338.   Kurian, George Thomas, ed. **World Education Encyclopedia**. New York: Facts on File, 1988. 3 vol. $195.00. LC: 82-18188. ISBN: 0-87196-748-0.

   Despite the publication date of this survey of education systems around the globe, it still contains significant information of use to researchers. Any information found, however, should be updated when possible by direct information from World Wide Web sites and other direct sources from the subject country. Because of constant changes in certain areas of the world, some of the countries included in this encyclopedia no longer exist and others have re-emerged to take their place. This major survey of education includes two weighty introductory pieces: one on world history and world education, and the other on statistical dimensions of global education. These are followed by entries for each country that include basic data, history and background, constitutional and legal background, and an overview of all levels of education. Other topics covered include administration, finance, educational research, nonformal education, the teaching profession, a summary, and a bibliography. The extent each country is described depends on the amount of available information. Useful, thorough resource.

339.   Postlethwaite, T. Neville, ed. **International Encyclopedia of National Systems of Education**. 2nd ed. Oxford, Eng.: Elsevier Science, 1995. 1,105 p. $263.75. LC: 95-34436. ISBN: 0-08-042302-7.

Overviews of 152 systems of education are presented in alphabetical arrangement from Afghanistan to Zimbabwe. Each entry includes general background information; politics and goals of the education system; the formal system of education; administrative structure; finance, personnel, curriculum, and teaching; graduation; assessment, reforms, and projections. A bibliography and suggestions for further reading are generally included with each entry. Contributors are usually from the country being described or are familiar with its educational system. A list of contributors and a name index are included. Helpful guide to national systems of education.

Directories and Almanacs

340.   **Advisory List of International Educational Travel and Exchange Programs, 1996-97**. Leesburg, Va.: Council on Standards for International Educational Travel (CSIET), 1996. 138 p. $8.50.

Advisory List serves as a guide to schools, prospective international high school students, and host families interested in educational travel or exchanges. The directory contains descriptions of programs that meet CSIET standards. Each description includes the countries or areas served, number of participants, and specific, although brief, details about the program. Also included in the directory are the standards established by CSIET for international educational travel programs. Useful and inexpensive guide for high school students exploring international educational travel programs.

341.   **International Study Telecom Directory**. Milwaukee, Wis.: World-Wide Classroom, 1998. 97 p. $15.00. ISBN: 1-1892242-00-1.

In 97 densely packed pages, this directory lists programs for international study around the globe. Listed alphabetically by country, and then in two categories, university and adult education, or K-12 and teen, each program listed includes the institution name, address, and telephone number. When available, FAX, e-mail, and Web addresses are provided. University and adult education programs include foreign language immersion institutes, universities, executive and business programs, internships, and cultural programs. K-12 and teen programs include teen camps, boarding schools, international schools, and teen exchange programs. Whether seeking an international primary school in Malaysia or an ESL program in Kentucky, this directory provides the information. Solid value is offered in this unique and compact directory.

342.   Steen, Sara J., ed. **Academic Year Abroad 1998/99**. 27th ed. New York: Institute of International Education, 1998. 692 p. $44.95. ISBN: 0-87206-241-4.

Subtitled "The Most Complete Guide to Planning Academic Year Study Abroad," this guide lists nearly 2,500 programs for the college student. Other learners may also be eligible for participation. Programs are arranged by geographical region, country, city, and institution. Each entry includes contact information, course credit, language of instruction, costs, subjects offered, housing, and application information. Indexes by sponsoring institutions, fields of study, consortial sponsors, special options for learners other than undergraduate students, cost ranges and duration of programs are included.

343.   **Study Abroad 1998-1999**. Paris: United Nations Educational, Scientific and Cultural Organization, International Bureau of Education, 1997. 1,215 p. $29.95. LC: 92-3-003401-0.

Published by UNESCO, with entries in English, French, or Spanish according to the official language of the corresponding country, this guide provides information on postsecondary education in most countries around the world. Additionally, information on scholarships, financial aid, admission requirements, and an application address are provided with each entry. International scholarships and courses offered by international organizations are listed first, followed by national scholarships and courses grouped by country. Indexes provide access by international organization, national institution, or subject of study. Valuable resource for international study options.

Guides, Handbooks, and Yearbooks

344.   Wickremasinghe, Walter, ed. **Handbook of World Education: A Comparative Guide to Higher Education and Educational Systems of the World**. Houston, Tex.: American Collegiate Service, 1992. 898 p. $98.00. LC: 90-080955. ISBN: 0-940937-03-4.

The *Handbook* presents major aspects of educational systems around the world in a single volume. Recognizing that trends and issues within education are as volatile as the political climate in the different countries, the editor presents this work as a snapshot of educational systems current at the time of publication. Notably, the reunification of Germany and the Persian Gulf War had an impact on the entries in this book. Each entry contains a background section, information on primary and secondary education, higher education, issues and trends, and a brief bibliography. The emphasis is on higher education, although lower levels are described as well. Each entry is written by an educator native to the country, and all have been translated into English. Useful brief overview of international education systems in a single volume.

Statistical Sources

345.   Davis, Todd M., ed. **Open Doors: Report on International Educa-tional Exchange 1996/1997**. New York: Institute of International Education, 1997. 208 p. $42.95. ISSN: 0078-5172. ISBN: 087206-243-0.

Open Doors remains the leading source of data related to foreign student enrollments, foreign scholars, and U.S. study abroad. Using graphs and charts, the data is presented in an easily understood format. Origin of students, institutions where enrolled, programs of study, and personal characteristics are some of the tables presented. Intensive English program enrollment and study abroad data for U.S. students are included. A data diskette is included.

346.   **Education at a Glance: OECD Indicators 1997**. http://www.oecd.org/els/stats/els_stat.htm. Paris: Organisation for Economic Co-operation and Development, 1997. 415 p. $50.00. ISBN: 92-64-15622-4.

Statistical data regarding the state of education in OECD countries is presented in this source with accompanying explanations. Comparisons are possible using this information in several categories such as student achievement, levels of education, work force outcomes of education, resources invested in education, access to education, and school organization. Appendixes include a glossary of terms, explanation of grade designations and ages in each country, basic reference statistics, and technical notes. The data underlying this report is available via the World Wide Web.

347.   **UNESCO Statistical Yearbook 1998**. Paris: United Nations Educational, Scientific and Cultural Organization, 1998. 1 vol. (various paging). $95.00. ISSN: 0082-7541. ISBN: 92-3-003562-9.

Extensive information about education and more limited information about science and technology, and culture and communication is presented in this international statistical compendium. Country comparisons are possible in areas such as literacy, enrollment, educational personnel, graduation, and public expenditures on education. This is an excellent source of statistical information related to education worldwide, and a critical resource for a collection with an international education focus.

348. **World Education Report 1993**. Paris: United Nations Educational, Scientific and Cultural Organization, 1993. 172 p. $35.00. ISBN: 92-3-103450-2.

Presents the major trends and policies in international education through statistical and narrative comparisons. The 1993 report specifically addresses information literacy and an increasing knowledge gap in a rapidly changing world, school choice issues, and educational standards. The appendixes report world education indicators for over 170 countries. Intended to be a biennial publication.

Journals

349. **Comparative Education**. Vol. 1-. Abingdon, Oxfordshire, Eng.: Carfax, 1965-. 3 issues per year. $570.00 (institutions). ISSN: 0305-0068.

Truly international in scope, this journal publishes educational studies that compare and analyze trends and issues across nations. Policy issues as they impact education and society in general are explored. Indexed in: *Current Index to Journals in Education, Social Sciences Citation Index.*

350. **Comparative Education Review**. Vol. 1-. Chicago: University of Chicago Press, 1957-. quarterly. $67.00. ISSN: 0010-4086.

As the official journal of the Comparative and International Education Society, *Comparative Education Review*, offers refereed articles that address multicultural, comparative, and international education concerns. Includes book reviews, an annual bibliography, and yearly special issue. Indexed in: *Current Index to Journals in Education, Education Index.*

351. **Compare: A Journal of Comparative Education**. Vol. 1-. Abingdon, Oxfordshire, Eng.: Carfax, 1971-. 3 issues per year. $468.00. ISSN: 0305-7925.

Focusing on comparisons of international education, this journal addresses research issues, policy concerns, and pedagogy within the context of political, social, and economic structures. Research articles, case studies, book reviews, and thematic issues are a regular part of the publication. Indexed in: *British Education Index, Educational Administration Abstracts, Linguistics and Language Behavior Abstracts, Multicultural Education Abstracts, Sociology of Education Abstracts, Special Educational Needs Abstracts.*

352. **Education and Society: International Journal in Education and Sociology**. Vol. 1-. Melbourne, Aus.: James Nicholas Publishers, 1983-. 2 issues per year. $95.00 (institutions). ISSN: 0726-2655.

With its focus on education and society, this journal offers an international perspective on sociocultural, economic, and political aspects of education. Current issues and problems confronting education and society are explored through research articles, reports of practice, brief research reports, and policy analyses. Book reviews are included. Indexed in: *Australian Education Index, Current Index to Journals in Education, Linguistics and Language Behavior Abstracts, Multicultural Education Abstracts.*

353. **European Education: A Journal of Translations**. Vol. 1-. Armonk, N.Y.: M. E. Sharpe, 1969-. quarterly. $506.00 (institutions). ISSN: 1056-4934.

Formerly *Western European Education*, this journal provides articles (translated to English when necessary) from leading journals in European countries, as well as research reports and documents from institutions and school agencies. All areas and levels of education are included. Indexed in: *Current Index to Journals in Education, Education Index, Psychological Abstracts, Sociology of Education Abstracts.*

354. **European Journal of Education: Research, Development and Policies**. Vol. 1-. Abingdon, Oxfordshire, Eng.: Carfax, 1964-. quarterly. $698.00 (institutions). ISSN: 0141-8211.

The official journal of the European Institute of Education and Social Policy publishes thematic issues on a quarterly basis. The focus is on educational policy and reform, developments in Western and Eastern European education, and comparative perspectives. This research journal is directed to educators and administrators at all educational levels and in a variety of educational and governmental settings. Indexed in: *British Education Index, Current Index to Journals in Education, Sociology of Education Abstracts.*

355. **International Journal of Educational Development**. Vol. 1-. New York: Elsevier Science, 1981-. bimonthly. $490.00 (institutions). ISSN: 0738-0593.

Development and reform within education around the globe, but particularly in developing countries, constitute the focus of this research journal. Literacy, adult education, training, economics of education, equity issues, and curricula are just a few of the areas addressed. Special attention is given to the impact of international aid and policy on developing countries and their educational systems and structures. Also includes book reviews. Indexed in: *Multicultural Education Abstracts, Research into Higher Education Abstracts, Social Sciences Citation Index, Sociology of Education Abstracts, Special Educational Needs Abstracts.*

10

CURRICULUM, INSTRUCTION, AND CONTENT AREAS

Dictionaries and Encyclopedias

356. Lewy, Arieh, ed. **The International Encyclopedia of Curriculum**. Oxford, Eng.: Pergamon, 1991. 1,064 p. (*Advances in Education*). $206.25. LC: 90-29143. ISBN: 0-80-041379-X. "Based on material from *The International Encyclopedia of Education*, first published 1985, with revisions and updated material."

This extensive collection of essays on international curricula was compiled for students, researchers, and scholars. The preface provides an overview of the history of curriculum studies and the organization of this book. Part 1 addresses curriculum as a domain of scholarly inquiry, with cross-curricular articles. Part 2 focuses not only on specific study areas dealing with subject and topical research, but also on areas considered less scholarly or more popular, such as daily living skills and media literacy. The volume includes a section on international curriculum associations and journals, as well as contributors, name, and subject indexes. As with the other works culled from *The International Encyclopedia of Education*, this spin-off provides an international cadre of experts writing on a particular aspect of education.

Directories and Almanacs

357. **El-Hi Textbooks and Serials in Print 1998**. 126th ed. New Providence, N.J.: R. R. Bowker, 1998. 2 vol. $149.00. LC: 70-105104. ISSN: 0000-0825. ISBN: 0-8352-4062-2.

Very similar to *Books in Print*, this directory to currently available textbooks, teaching materials, and other classroom materials in book form suitable for elementary and secondary education provides access to over 90,000 items. Audiovisual materials are not included unless they are part of a specific textbook program. Organized by subject, it is possible to browse through the publications in print under topics such as art, foreign languages, mathematics, and reading. Each item listed includes author, title, pagination, year of publication, cost, ISBN, and publisher. Entries are published in volume 1. Volume 2 contains indexes by author, title and series for books; by subject and title for serials; and a list of publishers and distributors with addresses and telecommunications information. Useful source for identifying textbook series, textbooks, and related classroom materials.

358. **Guidebook of Federal Resources for K-12 Mathematics and Science**. http://www.enc.org/about/index.htm. 4th ed. Columbus, Ohio: Eisenhower National Clearinghouse for Mathematics and Science Education, Ohio State University, 1997-98. 277 p. free.

Supported by the federal government, this directory provides information about federal offices, programs, and facilities supporting K-12 math and science education. In addition, federally funded programs in each state and territory are listed in a separate section. Also available electronically.

359. Miller, Elizabeth B. **Internet Resource Directory for K-12 Teachers and Librarians**. 1999/2000 ed. http://www.lu.com/Internet_ Resource_Directory. Englewood, Colo.: Libraries Unlimited, 1999. 460 p. $27.50. ISBN: 1-56308-718-9.

Organized by curriculum areas, the directory lists 1,497 entries that have been selected based on stated evaluative criteria, and includes state and national standards for education in content areas. Topic areas include resources for educators (including lesson plans across the curriculum), the arts, computer science, foreign languages, language arts, mathematics, science, applied arts and sciences, social studies and geography, and school library resources. Indexes provide access by subjects and site names. Each entry includes a brief annotation or, in the case of listservs, instructions for subscribing. Free monthly updates to the directory are available at the Web site listed above. Excellent directory to quality Internet sites for K-12 teachers, librarians, parents, and students.

Guides, Handbooks, and Yearbooks

360. Brown, David. **Goldmine, 1995-96: Finding Free and Low-Cost Resources for Teaching**. 5th ed. Brookfield, Vt.: Ashgate Publishing, 1993. 336 p. $27.95. ISBN: 1-85742-137-X.

This British-based guide is updated annually. Of primary interest to teachers seeking information about free and inexpensive classroom resources in the United Kingdom, it offers confirmation that teachers worldwide seek inexpensive supplemental classroom materials to bolster their curricula. Covers all subject areas and includes subject index and supplier lists.

361. **Educators Guide to Free Science Materials**. 39th ed. Randolph, Wis.: Educators Progress Service, 1998. 248 p. $27.95. LC: 61-919. ISBN: 0-87708-312-6.

With nearly 1,700 free titles listed, 559 of which are new to this edition, this guide fulfills its mission of listing classroom resources in a variety of formats for the busy and underfunded science teacher. Categories range from aerospace education to physics, and each section provides titles with full address and ordering information, suggested grade levels and, where available, e-mail, World Wide Web, and FAX numbers. Title, subject, and source indexes are included.

362. **Educators Guide to Free Social Studies Materials**. 38th ed. Randolph, Wis.: Educators Progress Service, 1998. 312 p. $29.95. LC: 61-65910. ISBN: 0-87708-313-4.

Citizenship, Communication and Transportation, Famous People, U.S. Geography, World Geography, Government, History, Maps, Social Problems, and World Affairs categorize the free K-12 classroom materials listed in this guide. Each entry includes a suggested grade level, brief description, and full ordering information including World Wide Web address when available. Over half of the 1,505 entries are new to this edition. Includes title, source, and subject indexes.

363. Gabel, Dorothy L., ed. **Handbook of Research on Science Teaching and Learning**. New York: Macmillan, 1994. 598 p. $75.00. LC: 93-17119. ISBN: 0-02-897005-5.

A project of the National Science Teachers Association, the handbook is directed to researchers, students, practitioners, and policy makers concerned with science education. Each of the extensively referenced contributions reviews and synthesizes research on a particular aspect of science education. Nineteen articles are presented in five categories: teaching, learning, problem solving, curriculum, and context. The handbook is useful as a historical overview, a report on current practice, and an indication of future directions. Name and subject indexes are included.

364.   **National Standard for Civics and Government**. Calabasas, Calif.: Center for Civic Education, 1994. 179 p. $12.00. ISBN: 0-89818-155-0.

Developed in response to the National Education Goals 2000, this set of standards focuses on content standards specifying what students should know and be able to do in the fields of civics and government. These standards are viewed as exit standards of what students should understand at the end of the 4th, 8th, and 12th grades. Course outlines are not provided. After an introductory overview, standards are presented for grades K-4, 5-8, and 9-12. Appendixes include organizational summaries of questions for each set of grades, a sample performance standard, glossary, acknowledgments, and an index.

365.   Pearson, P. David, Barr, Rebecca, Kamil, Michael L., and Mosenthal, Peter, ed. **Handbook of Reading Research**. New York: Longman, 1984, 1991. 2 vols. $70.95 (vol. 1); $109.95 (vol. 2). LC: 83-26838. ISBN: 0-582-28119-9 (vol. 1); 0-8013-0292-7 (vol. 2).

The two volumes of this impressive handbook contain extensively referenced articles on the field of reading. Rather than preparing a second edition of the *Handbook*, the editors developed a second volume which builds upon the first. While the topics of certain articles in the first volume may be repeated, they are not written by the same authors. Volume 1 contains articles about the history of reading research, methodological issues, and the state of reading processes and instructional practices. Volume 2 incorporates more articles on literacy, societal issues, and the schooling process as related to reading research. Both volumes feature contributors well known for their research in reading and literacy, and are well indexed. This is a staple source of information on reading and literacy.

366.   Perry, Phyllis J. **Guide to Math Materials: Resources to Support the NCTM Standards**. Englewood, Colo.: Teacher Ideas Press, 1997. 127 p. $20.00. LC: 96-33101. ISBN: 1-56308-491-0.

This guide to resource materials supports the curriculum standards developed by the National Council of Teachers of Mathematics (NCTM). Mathematics materials for grades K-4 are presented in thirteen chapters reflecting the thirteen math curriculum standards. Each chapter presents the standard, some background information, and a descriptive list of related classroom materials. Resources that are appropriate across the NCTM standards are also included. A list of suppliers and a subject index increase the usefulness of this work.

367. Seaton, Don Cash, Schmottlach, Neil, McManama, Jerre L., Clayton, Irene A., Leibee, Howard C., and Messersmith, Lloyd L. **Physical Education Handbook**. 8th ed. Englewood Cliffs, N.J.: Prentice Hall, 1992. 430 p. $47.00. LC: 91-24567. ISBN: 0-13-663097-9.

Useful to teachers, physical educators, youth group leaders, and others interested in sports activities and physical fitness, this handbook offers background information about physical education, specific skills for different activities, and how to conduct games and tournaments. Information about modifying activities for special populations is also included. Although it lacks an index, the table of contents provides quick access to activities such as badminton, dance, golf, recreational sports, and tennis. Each activity section also includes relevant terminology with definitions, selected references, and illustrations demonstrating techniques, rules, and equipment. Appendixes provide supplemental and further sources of information. Good source of physical education information.

368. **Secondary Teachers Guide to Free Curriculum Materials**. 107th ed. Randolph, Wis.: Educators Progress Service, 1998. 403 p. $47.95. LC: 44-32700. ISBN: 0-87708-317-7.

Formerly *Educators Index of Free Materials*, this guide lists free classroom materials for secondary schools in all subject areas, special education, teacher resources, and technology education. Educational resources for parents are also included. Over 1,100 of the 1,662 entries are new to this edition. Access is provided through subject, source, and title indexes. Full ordering information is included with each entry.

369. Shaver, James P., ed. **Handbook of Research on Social Studies Teaching and Learning**. New York: Macmillan, 1991. 661 p. $75.00. LC: 90-38751. ISBN: 0-02-895790-3.

A project of the National Council for the Social Studies, this handbook offers an overview of research in the social studies and its future direction. Directed to researchers and students, the contents discuss epistemology and methodology; students; teachers; contexts; teaching and learning outcomes; components of instruction; relationships with other curriculum areas; and international perspectives of social studies research. Individual articles within these categories address multicultural education, critical research, teacher competence, classroom discourse, and more as they relate to the social studies. Name and subject indexes provide access points not immediately apparent within the framework of the table of contents. Significant source of information on social studies research.

Indexes and Abstracts

370. **Business Education Index**. Little Rock, Ark.: Delta Pi Epsilon, National Honorary Professional Graduate Society in Business Education, 1940-. v. 57, 1996. Issued annually. $25.00. ISSN: 0068-4414.

The audience for this annual index includes researchers and teachers of business education with emphasis on information systems, business communications, business teacher education, marketing education, and vocational education. A very select list of business publications are indexed in this specialized reference tool. Rather than using a subject index, the arrangement is by subject categories and subcategories. It is possible for an article to be listed more than once (up to four times) depending on its focus. A separate author index is included. Suitable for collections with an emphasis on business and vocational education.

371. **Physical Education Index**. Vol. 1-. Cape Girardeau, Mo.: BenOak Publishing, 1978-. quarterly. $195.00. ISSN: 0191-9202.

Coverage of international journal literature dealing with dance, health, physical education, physical therapy, recreation, sports, sports medicine, and related areas is provided in this quarterly index. Teaching methods, training, and related education topics are included. Three issues per year are published in paperbound format; the fourth issue is a hardcover bound cumulation.

World Wide Web and Internet Sources

372. **Blue Web'n: A Library of Blue Ribbon Learning Sites on the Web**. http://www.kn.pacbell.com/wired/bluewebn/ (accessed February 28, 1999).

Blue Web'n is a searchable database of Internet sites with K-12 resources listed by subject area, audience, and type (lessons, activities, projects, resources, references, and tools). One of the extremely valuable aspects of this site is the way it provides background information and guides the user through the different features. Evaluative criteria are used before including a resource at this site. This is an excellent resource with options for being notified of new resources as they are added.

373. **GEM: The Gateway to Educational Materials**. http://www. thegateway.org (accessed December 14, 1998).

Sponsored by the U.S. Department of Education's National Library of Education, and as a special project of the ERIC Clearinghouse on Information and Technology, this site offers access to high quality education resources, including lesson plans and curriculum units. The options of browsing by keyword or subject lists or of doing a simple search make this a user-friendly resource. Search features include limiting by grade or educational level. With over 3,200 resources from a variety of participants, GEM provides lesson plans and other curriculum resources with clear objectives for every level of instruction.

374. **Learning Page: American Memory**. http://memory.loc.gov/ ammem/ndlpedu/index.html (accessed February 27, 1999).

Taken from primary source documents at the Library of Congress and elsewhere, and part of the American Memory project, the Learning Page offers digital versions of resources that can be used by students and educators to learn more about American history. Separate entry points for learners and for educators are provided. Lesson plans, thematic features, and more provide a wealth of resources with images and text. This is a valuable source for U.S. history and culture lessons.

Journals

375. **American Biology Teacher**. Vol. 1-. Reston, Va.: National Association of Biology Teachers, 1938-. 9 issues per year. $75.00 (institutions). ISSN: 0002-7685.

As the official journal of the National Association of Biology Teachers, a combination of research and hands-on classroom articles are presented, as well as regular features such as technology and book reviews. Indexed in: *Current Index to Journals in Education, Education Index, Social Sciences Citation Index.*

376. **Art Education**. Vol. 1-. Reston, Va.: National Art Education Association, 1948-. bimonthly. $50.00 (nonmembers). ISSN: 0004-3125.

The National Art Education Association incorporates current issues and research, classroom practice, historical studies and association information in its official bimonthly publication. Indexed in: *Current Index to Journals in Education, Education Index*.

377. **Communication Education**. Vol. 1-. Annandale, Va.: National Communication Association, 1952-. quarterly. $100.00 (institutions). ISSN: 0363-4523.

Articles deal with instruction in traditional classroom settings as well as less traditional environments. Communication instruction, development of communication skills, and communication within the context of instruction are the primary focus. Formerly *Speech Teacher.* Indexed in: *Current Index to Journals in Education*.

378. **Curriculum Inquiry**. Vol. 1-. Malden, Mass.: Blackwell, 1971-. quarterly. $116.50 (institutions). ISSN: 0362-6784.

Formerly: *Curriculum Theory Network*. Affiliated with the Ontario Institute for Studies in Education, this journal provides research and essay articles about curricula, teaching, classroom practices, and educational change. Book reviews are also included. Indexed in: *Canadian Education Index, Current Index to Journals in Education, Education Index, Multicultural Education Abstracts, Research into Higher Education Abstracts, Social Sciences Citation Index, Sociology of Education Abstracts*.

379. **Curriculum Review: A Monthly Report on What Works in Our Schools**. Vol. 1-. Metuchen, N.J.: WD&S Publishing, 1960-. 9 issues per year. $89.00. ISSN: 0147-2453.

Brief reports of current trends in K-12 education appear in this publication as do software and textbook reviews, successful classroom activities, and opinion pieces. Includes useful information for the practitioner as well as a monthly report on controversial issues within schools. Indexed in: *Contents Pages in Education, Education Index*.

380. **English Education: Official Journal of the Conference on English Education**. Vol. 1-. Urbana, Ill.: National Council of Teachers of English (NCTE), 1969-. quarterly. $30.00 (institutions). ISSN: 0007-8204.

Published for the Conference on English Education by NCTE, this slim publication offers research and practice articles on the teaching of English and language arts, and especially of the training and development of those who will teach in these areas. Indexed in: *Current Index to Journals in Education, Education Index, Social Sciences Citation Index.*

381. **English Journal**. Vol. 1-. Urbana, Ill.: National Council of Teachers of English (NCTE), 1912-. bimonthly. $60.00 (institutions). ISSN: 0013-8274.

Focusing on language and literature at the secondary level, this journal uses thematic issues to address topics such as gender in the curriculum, research papers, and writing. NCTE news, practical classroom ideas, book reviews, and reviews of young adult literature are regularly included as well as research and essay articles. Indexed in: *Current Index to Journals in Education, Education Index, Exceptional Child Education Resources, Social Sciences Citation Index.*

382. **For the Learning of Mathematics: An International Journal of Mathematics Education**. Vol. 1-. Kingston, Ont., Canada: FLM Publishing Association, 1980-. 3 issues per year. $42.00 (institutions). ISSN: 0228-0671.

Research articles, reports of research projects, and research reviews that impact on the learning of mathematics are presented in this internationally focused journal. Indexed in: *Current Index to Journals in Education.*

383. **History Teacher**. Vol. 1-. Long Beach, Calif.: California State University, Long Beach, 1967-. quarterly. $55.00 (institutions). ISSN: 0018-2745.

Published in affiliation with the American Historical Association and the Society for History Education, this journal offers research and essay articles on historical research and the teaching of history, as well as reviews of relevant textbooks, media, and professional books. Indexed in: *Current Index to Journals in Education, Education Index.*

384. **International Journal of Science Education**. Vol. 1-. London: Taylor & Francis, 1979-. 10 issues per year. $695.00 (institutions). ISSN: 0950-0693.

Truly international in scope, this journal provides refereed articles which have a research base with practical applications. Book reviews, research reports, reports on new approaches and developments within science education, and general articles related to science teaching and learning are presented. Indexed in: *Current Index to Journals in Education, Education Index, Research into Higher Education Abstracts, Social Sciences Citation Index.*

385.   **Journal for Research in Mathematics Education**. http://www. nctm.org/jrme/. Vol. 1-. Reston, Va.: National Council of Teachers of Mathematics (NCTM), 1970-. 5 issues per year. $57.00 (members). ISSN: 0021-8251.

Book reviews, research articles, case studies, commentaries, and surveys related to mathematics education at all levels appear in this NCTM publication. Valuable source of research related to the teaching and learning of mathematics. Other NCTM publications address practice and classroom strategies. Also available electronically. Indexed in: *Current Index to Journals in Education, Education Index, Psychological Abstracts, Social Sciences Citation Index.*

386.   **Journal of Adolescent & Adult Literacy**. Vol. 1- . Newark, Del.: International Reading Association, 1957-. 8 issues per year. $45.00. ISSN: 1081-3004.

Formerly *Journal of Developmental Reading* and the *Journal of Reading*, this journal includes research, theory, and practice articles related to reading instruction. Regular features include reviews of classroom and professional materials and books for young adults. The focus is on both adolescent and adult literacy within the school setting and beyond. Indexed in: *Current Index to Journals in Education, Education Index, Exceptional Child Education Abstracts, Social Sciences Citation Index.*

387.   **Journal of Aesthetic Education**. Vol. 1-. Champaign, Ill.: University of Illinois Press, 1966-. quarterly. $50.00 (institutions). ISSN: 0021-8510.

Research articles and book reviews related to aesthetic education and to the issues of aesthetics in society as a whole are the focus of this journal. Instruction, learning, and an understanding of aesthetics within all levels of education form the core topics addressed. Indexed in: *Current Journals in Education, Education Index, Psychological Abstracts, Social Sciences Citation Index.*

388.   **Journal of Alcohol and Drug Education**. Vol. 1-. Lansing, Mich.: American Alcohol and Drug Information Foundation, 1955-. 3 issues per year. $45.00. ISSN: 0090-1482.

Serving as a voice for alcohol and drug education research, classroom education strategies, and new prevention programs, this journal also presents differing points of view. Most articles are research-based and address alcohol, tobacco, and drug use within all levels of educational settings. Indexed in: *Current Index to Journals in Education, Education Index, Higher Education Abstracts, Multicultural Education Abstracts, Psychological Abstracts, Social Sciences Citation Index.*

389. **Journal of Curriculum and Supervision**. Vol. 1-. Alexandria, Va.: Association for Supervision and Curriculum Development (ASCD), 1985-. quarterly. $44.00 (nonmembers). ISSN: 0882-1232.

Scholarly articles that explore and reflect curriculum and supervision practices and policies are presented in the pages of this ASCD publication. Speculative, historical, and analytical approaches are welcomed as they relate to teaching, learning, and leadership within curriculum and supervision. Indexed in: *Current Index to Journals in Education, Education Index, Sociology of Education Abstracts.*

390. **Journal of Curriculum Studies** . Vol. 1-. London: Taylor & Francis, 1968-. bimonthly. $311.00 (institutions). ISSN: 0022-0272.

Opinion pieces, research and historical articles, and essay and book reviews form the contents of this internationally-focused journal. Innovations, analyses, content area studies, reform issues, and implications for practice within the area of curriculum studies are addressed. Also available electronically. Indexed in: *Current Index to Journals in Education, Education Index, Educational Administration Abstracts, Linguistics and Language Behavior Abstracts, Multicultural Education Abstracts, Social Sciences Citation Index, Sociology of Education Abstracts.*

391. **Journal of Experiential Education**. Vol. 1-. Boulder, Colo.: Association for Experiential Education, 1978-. 3 issues per year. $25.00. ISSN: 1053-8259.

Of the three issues published annually, one has a general focus while the other two are thematic. All deal with experiential learning, and frequently address adventure-based learning. Descriptive and research articles and brief research updates are included. Indexed in: *Current Index to Journals in Education.*

392. **Journal of Research in Science Teaching**. Vol. 1-. New York: John Wiley & Sons, 1963-. 10 issues per year. $650.00 (institutions). ISSN: 0022-4308.

The official journal of the National Association for Research in Science Teaching provides a forum for scholarly articles and commentaries on science instruction at all educational levels. Research articles range from ethnographic studies to literature reviews. Also available electronically. Indexed in: *Current Index to Journals in Education, Education Index, Educational Technology Abstracts, Multicultural Education Abstracts, Psychological Abstracts, Social Sciences Citation Index, Sociology of Education Abstracts.*

393.   **Language Arts**. Vol. 1-. Urbana, Ill.: National Council of Teachers of English (NCTE), 1924-. bimonthly. $60.00 (institutions). ISSN: 0360-9170.

Previously published as *Elementary English*, this NCTE journal focuses on preschool through middle grade school age children and their learning language arts. Articles also address teaching language arts in the school. Research articles, commentaries, association news, and book reviews are regularly included. Indexed in: *Current Index to Journals in Education, Education Index, Linguistics and Language Behavior Abstracts.*

394.   **Montessori Life**. Vol. 1-. New York: American Montessori Society, 1981-. quarterly. $30.00. ISSN: 1054-0040.

Promoting the philosophy of the American Montessori Society (AMS), *Montessori Life* offers articles on curricula, classified ads of Montessori-appropriate products, book reviews, teacher profiles, and AMS news. Indexed in: *Current Index to Journals in Education.*

395.   **Reading and Writing Quarterly: Overcoming Learning Difficulties**. Vol. 1-. London: Taylor & Francis, 1984-. quarterly. $215.00 (institutions). ISSN: 1057-3569.

Previously *Chicorel Abstracts on Reading and Learning Disabilities* and *Journal of Reading, Writing, and Learning Disabilities International*, this former abstracting service is now a refereed journal. The focus is on diagnosis, prevention, and improvement of reading and writing difficulties in both regular and special education settings. Indexed in: *Current Index to Journals in Education, Exceptional Child Education Resources, Linguistics and Language Behavior Abstracts, Psychological Abstracts.*

396.   **Reading Horizons**. Vol. 1-. Kalamazoo, Mich.: College of Education, Western Michigan University, 1960-. quarterly. $25.00 (institutions). ISSN: 0034-0502.

Original research reports, theoretical articles, essays, policy analyses, and reviews of children's literature are included in this publication. The focus is on reading, literacy, and the language arts. Indexed in: *Current Index to Journals in Education, Education Index.*

397. **Reading Improvement**. Vol. 1-. Mobile, Ala.: Project Innovation, 1963-. quarterly. $30.00 (institutions). ISSN: 0034-0510.

Focusing on the teaching of reading and the improvement of that process, this journal presents theoretical and applied research articles. All levels of reading instruction are addressed. Indexed in: *Current Index to Journals in Education, Education Index, Linguistics and Language Behavior Abstracts.*

398. **Reading Research and Instruction**. Vol. 1-. Carrollton, Ga.: College Reading Association, 1961-. quarterly. $50.00. ISSN: 0886-0246.

Formerly *Reading World*, this publication of the College Reading Association offers scholarly articles on reading instruction, practices in literacy education, and applied research in reading. Indexed in: *Current Index to Journals in Education, Education Index, Psychological Abstracts, Social Sciences Citation Index.*

399. **Reading Research Quarterly**. Vol. 1-. Newark, Del.: International Reading Association, 1965-. quarterly. $45.00. ISSN: 0034-0553.

Book reviews, commentaries, and research and theoretical articles related to reading and literacy education appear in this refereed journal. Research as it affects practice is a strong theme in the articles. Indexed in: *Current Index to Journals in Education, Education Index.*

400. **Reading Teacher**. Vol. 1-. Newark, Del.: International Reading Association, 1951-. 8 issues per year. $90.00 (institutions). ISSN: 0034-0561.

Focused on reading and literacy learning, this journal incorporates reviews of children's books, research, theory and practice articles, essays, and program and practice reports. Indexed in: *Current Index to Journals in Education, Education Index, Exceptional Child Education Resources, Multicultural Education Abstracts, Psychological Abstracts, Social Sciences Citation Index, Special Educational Needs Abstracts.*

401.   **Religious Education**. Vol. 1-. Atlanta, Ga.: Religious Education
Association, 1906-. quarterly. $70.00 (institutions). ISSN: 0034-
4087.

Interdisciplinary, interfaith, and international in scope, this
well-established journal explores spirituality and religion in education through scholarly and practice articles; essays; and reviews
of books, media, and curricula. Both independent and state-sponsored
educational institutions are considered as are informal programs at
all levels of education. Indexed in: *Current Index to Journals in
Education, Education Index, Psychological Abstracts, Social Sciences Citation Index.*

402.   **Research in the Teaching of English**. http://www.ncte.org/rte/.
Vol. 1-. Urbana, Ill.: National Council of Teachers of English
(NCTE), 1967-. quarterly. $30.00 (institutions). ISSN: 0034-527X.

In addition to the research and scholarly articles on language
teaching and learning at all levels, this NCTE publication also
issues supplemental and complementary material on the World
Wide Web. Language arts and reading from preschool through adult
levels are addressed. Also includes a periodically published annotated bibliography of research materials related to the teaching of
English. Indexed in: *Current Index to Journals in Education, Education Index, Linguistics and Language Behavior Abstracts, Multicultural Education Abstracts, Social Sciences Citation Index.*

403.   **School Arts**. Vol. 1-. Worcester, Mass.: Davis Publications, 1901-.
9 issues per year. $24.50. ISSN: 0036-6463.

Practical classroom activities, suggestions for field trips, book
and media reviews, teaching tips, and suggestions for curriculum
enhancements abound in this appropriately colorful art education
journal. A quick guide to articles and features of interest to specific
grades is included. Indexed in: *Current Index to Journals in
Education.*

404.   **Science and Children**. Vol. 1-. Arlington, Va.: National Science
Teachers Association (NSTA), 1963-. monthly. $70.00 (institu-
tions). ISSN: 0036-8148.

Directed to elementary teachers, this NSTA publication offers
classroom activities, posters, lesson plans, and practical articles on
bringing science into the classroom. Reviews of classroom and
professional materials, software, and children's books appear regularly. Valuable resource for the busy science teacher. Indexed in:
*Current Index to Journals in Education, Education Index, Excep-
tional Child Education Resources.*

405.   **Science Education**. Vol. 1-. New York: John Wiley & Sons, 1916-.
6 issues per year. $565.00 (institutions). ISSN: 0036-8326.

International in scope and focused on research articles, this
journal addresses science instruction and learning at all levels of
education. Indexed in: *Current Index to Journals in Education,
Education Index, Psychological Abstracts, Social Sciences Citation
Index.*

406.   **Science Scope**. Vol. 1-. Arlington, Va.: National Science Teachers
Association (NSTA), 1978-. 8 issues per year. $70.00 (institutions).
ISSN: 0887-2376.

One of NSTA's practice-oriented journals, this one is directed
to middle and junior high school science teachers. Includes association information, book and media reviews, classroom activities,
and information about events and resources of value to busy classroom teachers. Indexed in: *Current Index to Journals in Education,
Education Index.*

407.   **Science Teacher**. Vol. 1-. Arlington, Va.: National Science Teachers
Association (NSTA), 1934-. 9 issues per year. $70.00 (institutions).
ISSN: 0036-8555.

This NSTA journal is directed to secondary science teachers
and includes articles describing effective practices, classroom activities, and teaching techniques. Also includes book reviews and
information about free and inexpensive resources. Indexed in: *Current Index to Journals in Education, Education Index.*

408.   **Social Education**. Vol. 1-. Washington, D.C.: National Council for
the Social Studies, 1937-. 7 issues per year. $59.00 (institutions).
ISSN: 0037-7724.

As the official journal of the National Council for the Social
Studies, this publication is a valuable source of information and
teaching activities for the social studies teacher. One of the regular
features is "teaching with documents" that takes source documents
from the National Archives and Records Administration to develop
teaching units with reproducibles. In one issue with a thematic
focus on immigration, the naturalization application for Archibald
Leach (Cary Grant) is reproduced and compared to current immigration procedures. Indexed in: *Current Index to Journals in Education, Education Index, Multicultural Education Abstracts, Social
Sciences Citation Index.*

409.   **Social Studies**. Vol. 1-. Washington, D.C.: Heldref, 1909-. bimonthly. $64.00 (institutions). ISSN: 0037-7996.

Refereed articles dealing with social studies, social sciences, history, and interdisciplinary studies appear in this journal. Social studies within the curriculum, learning strategies, historical issues, and current topics are considered. Indexed in: *Current Index to Journals in Education, Education Index, Social Sciences Citation Index, Special Educational Needs Abstracts.*

410.   **Theory and Research in Social Education**. Vol. 1-. Washington, D.C.: College and University Faculty Assembly of National Council for the Social Studies, 1972-. quarterly. $39.00 (institutions). ISSN: 0093-3104.

Focusing on research in social education, this journal emphasizes the relationship between education and schooling to society and social change. Conceptual and empirical studies are included as are relevant book reviews. Indexed in: *Current Index to Journals in Education, Education Index, Multicultural Education Abstracts, Psychological Abstracts, Social Sciences Citation Index, Sociology of Education Abstracts.*

11

EDUCATIONAL ADMINISTRATION AND MANAGEMENT

Guides, Handbooks, and Yearbooks

411.   Firth, Gerald R., and Pajak, Edward F., ed. **Handbook of Research on School Supervision**. New York: Simon & Schuster Macmillan, 1998. 1,298 p. $95.00. LC: 97-36964. ISBN: 0-02-864662-2.

Substantial in size and substantive in content, this handbook provides an overview of school supervision, its history, trends, practice, philosophy, and future. The handbook is divided into nine sections with 52 chapters. The nine sections address supervision as a field of inquiry; foundations; its professional practice; specialized areas; levels of education where practiced; relationships to allied areas; as an organized profession; theories; and forces, factors, and the future. Name and subject indexes offer additional points of access.

412.   Thrasher, Michele, ed. **Education Laws: A Compilation of Statutes in Effect Today**. 4th ed. Alexandria, Va.: Capitol Publications, 1992. 657 p. $112.00. ISBN: 0-937925-95-0.

This compilation of education laws makes it easy to identify federal legislation affecting education. Federal laws governing programs administered by the U.S. Department of Education are contained in this resource. Each law includes any amendments incorporated into the text, making it easy to follow the sense of the legislation. Divided into five categories, general education, elementary and secondary education, special education, vocational and technical education, and higher education, this source provides access to key mandates in these areas. A very brief index to laws by title is provided. Although rather outdated, this is still a useful guide to legislation that affects education programs and services.

Indexes and Abstracts

413.   **Educational Administration Abstracts**. Vol. 1-. Thousand Oaks, Calif.: Corwin Press, 1966-. quarterly. $355.00 (institutions). ISSN: 0013-1601.

Drawing from professional books, journals, and related resources in the field of educational administration, this abstracting service provides summaries of each item. Categories such as administrative structure, personnel, professional and staff development, and school business and finance are used to group abstracted items together, making it easy for researchers to browse through areas of interest. Author and subject indexes provide more traditional forms of access. Useful for specialized searching of the educational administration literature.

Journals

414.   **Economics of Education Review**. Vol. 1-. Exeter, Eng.: Elsevier Science, 1982-. quarterly. $372.00 (institutions). ISSN: 0272-7757.

International in scope, the focus of this publication is on the relationship between education and economics. All aspects of the economics of education are explored in research articles and policy analyses. These range from earnings based on educational levels to the social benefits of education. Book and literature reviews are also published. Indexed in: *Current Index to Journals in Education, Higher Education Abstracts, Multicultural Education Abstracts, Sociology of Education Abstracts.*

415.   **Educational Administration Quarterly**. Vol. 1-. Thousand Oaks, Calif.: Corwin Press, 1964-. 5 times per year. $275.00 (institutions). ISSN: 0013-161X.

Sponsored by the University Council for Educational Administration, this journal maintains a scholarly focus on educational administration, administrator education and training, and education reform. Research articles, policy analyses, research reviews and methodological analyses are included. Quarterly issues and an annual supplement are published. Indexed in: *Current Index to Journals in Education, Education Index, Educational Administration Abstracts, Multicultural Education Abstracts, Social Sciences Citation Index, Sociology of Education Abstracts.*

416. **High School Magazine for Principals, Assistant Principals, and All High School Leaders**. Vol. 1-. Reston, Va.: National Association of Secondary School Principals (NASSP), 1993-. 7 issues per year. $25.00 (NASSP members). ISSN: 1070-9533.

This NASSP publication provides practical guidance for the high school administrator. Whether the topic is educational standards, current legislation, new technologies, or immigrant students, useful tactics and successful practices are presented and explored. Regular features include book reviews, opposing viewpoint commentaries, and association information.

417. **Journal of Education Finance**. Vol. 1-. Reston, Va.: Association of School Business Officials International, 1975-. quarterly. $60.00 (institutions). ISSN: 0098-9495.

Book reviews and scholarly articles related to education finance are presented in this publication. Theory and practice are explored in articles addressing areas such as the correlation between spending and student achievement, school vouchers, and equity issues. Indexed in: *Current Index to Journals in Education, Education Index, Educational Administration Abstracts, Higher Education Abstracts*.

418. **Journal of Educational Administration**. Vol. 1-. Birmingham, Ala.: MCB University Press, 1963-. quarterly. $1,549.00. ISSN: 0957-8234.

All aspects of educational administration at different levels of education are explored in research and practice articles in this internationally-focused publication. Whether dealing with organizational issues, administrator or teacher burnout, or leadership development, the contents address some of the leading issues confronting educational administrators. Book reviews are included. Also available electronically. Indexed in: *Australian Education Index, Current Index to Journals in Education, Educational Administration Abstracts, Multicultural Education Abstracts, Research into Higher Education Abstracts, Social Sciences Citation Index, Sociology of Education Abstracts*.

419. **NASSP Bulletin**. Vol. 1-. Reston, Va.: National Association of Secondary School Principals (NASSP), 1917-. 9 issues per year. $110.00 (institutions). ISSN: 0192-6365.

Articles that are research-based and/or that have implications for practice for middle school and high school administrators and book reviews are featured in this association publication. All aspects of school administration are covered, such as leadership development, technology, and school community relations. Indexed in: *Current Index to Journals in Education, Education Index, Exceptional Child Education Resources, Multicultural Education Abstracts, Sociology of Education Abstracts.*

420.   **Principal**. Vol. 1-. Alexandria, Va.: National Association of Elementary School Principals (NAESP), 1921-. 5 issues per year. $115.00 (institutions). ISSN: 0271-6062.

Association news, book reviews, legal case studies, and articles of value to elementary and middle school administrators and educators are presented. Topics include parent-school interactions, special needs students, public perceptions of schooling, and other policy issues. Also available electronically. Indexed in: *Current Index to Journals in Education, Education Index, Exceptional Child Education Resources.*

421.   **School Administrator**. Vol. 1-. Arlington, Va.: American Association of School Administrators (AASA), 1943-. 11 issues per year. $40.00. ISSN: 0036-6439.

School system administrators and superintendents will benefit from the practical articles in this AASA journal. Association news, book reviews, and federal legislative updates are regularly featured. Topics addressed in articles include school board interactions, dismissals, and nontraditional (non-educator) superintendents. Also available electronically. Indexed in: *Current Index to Journals in Education, Education Index.*

422.   **State Education Leader**. Vol. 1-. Denver, Colo.: Education Commission of the States, 1966-. 3 issues per year. $20.00. ISSN: 0736-7511.

Practical articles and information about education issues within various states are presented in each issue of this journal. Useful tool for state leaders concerned with educational policy, reform, and administration. Indexed in: *Education Index, Exceptional Child Education Resources.*

12

EDUCATIONAL HISTORY
AND PHILOSOPHY

Dictionaries and Encyclopedias

423. Chambliss, J. J., ed. **Philosophy of Education: An Encyclopedia**. New York: Garland Publishing, 1996. 720 p. (*Garland Reference Library of the Humanities* v. 1,671). $100.00. LC: 96-18393. ISBN: 0-8153-1177-X.

    Relatively brief articles on all aspects of the philosophy of education are contained in this unique encyclopedia. With 228 articles, some of which are extensive in their coverage, such as overviews of the history of educational philosophy, this work provides keys to the major figures in educational philosophy, the differing philosophical systems, and the impact of philosophy on education. To that end, articles on Plato, Jane Addams, and Gandhi co-exist in a coherent framework of educational issues. Well-referenced articles address not only the historical significance of philosophical beliefs, but also the affect on society and educational institutions and policies. Since the encyclopedia lacks a table of contents or headings on each page, the extensive subject index is critical in locating information.

424. Raffel, Jeffrey A. **Historical Dictionary of School Segregation and Desegregation: The American Experience**. Westport, Conn.: Greenwood Press, 1998. 345 p. $75.00. LC: 98-11102. ISBN: 0-313-29502-6.

More than a dictionary, this work chronicles the history of school segregation and desegregation through a cogent introduction, a chronology of events from 1787 to 1996, a dictionary of terms and key figures, a bibliographical essay, and general and geographical bibliographies. The dictionary comprises the majority of the text, and essays of varying length describe terms, laws, individuals, and desegregation policies related to school segregation and desegregation. Although the focus is historical, events as current as the mid-1990s are included when relevant. References for further information are appended to each essay. A lengthy index provides enhanced access to the contents. Excellent reference source on these topics.

Directories and Almanacs

425. Caspard, Pierre, ed. **International Guide for Research in the History of Education**. 2nd ed. Bern, Switzerland: Peter Lang, 1995. 275 p. ISBN: 3-906754-27-8.

Sponsored by the International Standing Conference for the History of Education (ISCHE), and published in collaboration with the Institut national de recherche pedagogique in Paris, this guide lists sources for research in the history of education in thirty-one countries. Although international in scope, the emphasis is strongly European and the contents are written in English or French. Each country's entry includes the following information: research centers or associations specializing in the history of education, chairs in the history of education, other resources specializing in the history of education (libraries, school museums, and electronic databases), reference books, and other useful information. For the researcher interested in exploring the history of education in a particular part of the world, this is an extremely valuable guide. Also included are author and name indexes, a bibliography, and a list of five international associations focused on the history of education.

426. **History of Education Museums and Collections International Directory**. DeKalb, Ill.: Blackwell History of Education Research Collection, Northern Illinois University, 1993. 135 p. $20.00.

Issued approximately every five years, the directory provides listings of international collections of use to educational historians, scholars, and researchers. Small private collections as well as university research collections are represented among the twenty-six countries included in the 1993 edition. A separate listing of nearly 1,200 American country schools appears at the back of the

volume. Useful directory for anyone seeking collections of historical textbooks, classroom equipment, and other educational publications and resources.

World Wide Web and Internet Sources

427. **History of Education Site**. http://www.socsci.kun.nl/ped/whp/
      histeduc/ (accessed February 27, 1999).

      This extensive, high-quality site offers links to other relevant
      sites internationally, provides background information about its
      purpose and contents, and provides access to actual texts and
      sources related to the history of education and childhood. Award
      winning and filled with interesting and graphically rich pages, the
      contents cover all aspects of education and childhood from a historical
      perspective to particular aspects of U.S. education during specific
      centuries. Of note is the inclusion of historical information about
      education, schools, and educators in countries around the globe. Links
      to research organizations concerned with the history of education and
      to archives, special collections, and school museums are also included.
      This is a truly rich and distinctive site for study and research related
      to the history of education and childhood.

Journals

428. **Educational Philosophy and Theory**. Vol. 1-. Abingdon, Oxford-
      shire, Eng.: Carfax, 1969-. 3 issues per year. $188.00 (institutions).
      ISSN: 0013-1857.

      Articles addressing contemporary issues in educational policy
      and politics as well as historical and classical philosophical studies
      and texts are included in this research journal. Book reviews,
      commentaries, and essays are also presented. Theory, philosophy,
      and policy related to education are the key themes. Indexed in:
      Australian Education Index, Educational Administration Abstracts.

429. **Educational Studies: A Journal in the Foundations of Educa-
      tion**. Vol. 1-. Ypsilanti, Mich.: American Educational Studies Asso-
      ciation, 1970-. quarterly. $30.00 (institutions). ISSN: 0013-1946.

      Formerly a journal comprised of scholarly book and media
      reviews, the format as of 1997 changed to include research articles
      related to the foundations of education. Educational philosophy,
      history, and studies are addressed in both articles and reviews.
      Indexed in: *Education Index, Psychological Abstracts, Social Sci-
      ences Citation Index.*

430. **Educational Theory**. Vol. 1-. Champaign, Ill.: University of Illinois Press, 1951-. quarterly. $30.00 (institutions). ISSN: 0013-2004.

Sponsored by several educational history and philosophy societies, notably the John Dewey Society and the Philosophy of Education Society, this journal provides a forum for research and essay articles that relate to the history, foundations, culture of education, and its philosophical underpinnings. Also includes book reviews. Indexed in: *Current Index to Journals in Education, Education Index, Multicultural Education Abstracts, Social Sciences Citation Index, Sociology of Education Abstracts.*

431. **History of Education**. Vol. 1-. London: Taylor & Francis, 1972-. quarterly. $390.00 (institutions). ISSN: 0046-760X.

The official journal of the History of Education Society is issued quarterly. International in focus, the articles primarily address educational history in the United Kingdom and its former colonies. Research papers and book reviews are included, often with appropriate photographs and illustrations. Also available electronically. Indexed in: *Current Index to Journals in Education, Education Index, Historical Abstracts, Paedogogica Historica, Research into Higher Education Abstracts.*

432. **History of Education Quarterly**. Vol. 1-. Slippery Rock, Pa.: History of Education Society, College of Education, Slippery Rock University, 1961-. quarterly. $57.00 (institutions). ISSN: 0018-2680.

This quarterly publication presents articles, reports, documents, essay reviews, and book and media reviews related to the history of education and childhood. All time periods are covered and the scope is international. Indexed in: *Current Index to Journals in Education, Education Index, Research Into Higher Education Abstracts, Social Sciences Citation Index.*

433. **Paedagogica Historica: International Journal of the History of Education**. Vol. 1-. Ghent, Belgium: Center for the Study of the History of Education, University of Ghent, 1961-. 3 issues per year. $84.00 (institutions). ISSN: 0030-9230.

Articles in English, French, and German related to the history of education appear in this truly international journal. In addition to historical research articles, extensive book reviews are included, as are reports of conferences, announcements of upcoming conferences, and tables of contents from other history of education journals. Extremely valuable for the serious researcher of the history of education. Indexed in: *British Education Index, Current Index to*

Journals in Education, Research into Higher Education Abstracts, Sociology of Education Abstracts.

434. **Studies in Philosophy and Education**. Vol. 1-. Dordrecht, The Netherlands: Kluwer Academic, 1960-. 6 issues per year. $290.00 (institutions). ISSN: 0039-3746.

Philosophical issues in educational research, policy, and practice are addressed in this journal. A variety of philosophical stances are presented. Book review essays and an occasional thematic issue are also offered. Indexed in: *Australian Education Index, Higher Education Abstracts, Sociology of Education Abstracts.*

Biographies

435. Gutek, Gerald L. **Cultural Foundations of Education: A Biographical Introduction**. New York: Macmillan, 1991. 407 p. $46.00. LC: 90-31846. ISBN: 0-02-348371-7.

Portraying eighteen prominent historical figures from Plato to W. E. B. DuBois, this text discusses their effect on the cultural foundations of education. Each chapter presents the historical context, an educational biography, the development of educational ideas, and an assessment of significance. Not all the figures described are traditionally considered to be educators, but the author makes compelling links to educational impact. Each chapter concludes with references, discussion questions, and suggested research topics. An index supplements the text. Useful as both a source of biographical information and a text on educational history and philosophy.

13

EDUCATIONAL RESEARCH, MEASUREMENT, AND TESTING

Dictionaries and Encyclopedias

436. Alkin, Marvin C., ed. **Encyclopedia of Educational Research**. 6th cd. New York: Macmillan, 1992. 4 vol. $546.25. LC: 91-38682. ISBN: 0-02-900431-4.

   This encyclopedia is an indispensable resource for any education collection dealing with research issues and methods. Sponsored by the American Educational Research Association, with an impressive list of contributors, the contents include both background information about various topics within education and articles about conducting research. The four volumes of the encyclopedia are alphabetically arranged within sixteen broad areas, such as the context of education, educational measurement and assessment, teaching, and instructional systems and strategies. Of particular interest may be the section on methods of inquiry, which includes articles on research methods and design. Each article includes references, and an extensive index provides subject and author access to the contents of the encyclopedia.

Directories and Almanacs

437. Conoley, Jane Close, and Impara, James C., ed. **Mental Measurements Yearbook**. http://ericae.net/scripts/trev3.asp. 12th ed. Lincoln, Nebr. Buros Institute of Mental Measurements, 1995. 1,259 p. $60.00. LC: 39-3422. ISBN: 910674-40-X. *The Supplement to the Twelfth Mental Measurements Yearbook* (440 p.) was published in

1996 with the same editors and publisher. Viewed as a bridge between editions of the *MMY*, the supplements contain reviews of new or significantly revised tests issued since publication of the last *Yearbook*.

Since the initial publication of the *MMY* in 1938, the *Yearbooks* have been viewed as the primary source of critical information about commercially published tests. Entries for each test include brief descriptive data, critiques, and bibliographies. Critiques of each test are written by experts in the field. The often extensive bibliographies appended to each entry relate to the construction, validity, and use of tests in different settings with different populations. Indexes provide access to publisher addresses, acronyms, titles, subjects, reviewers and authors, and trait being measured. Portions of this data are also available through the World Wide Web.

438.   **ETS Test Collection Catalog**. http://www.ericae.net/testcol.htm. Phoenix, Ariz.: Oryx Press, 1986-1993. 6 vol. $55.00 (vol. 1, 1993). LC: 86-678. ISBN: 0-89774-743-7 (vol. 1).

Drawn from the 18,000 tests and measures in the Test Collection at Educational Testing Service (ETS), this set of directories lists tests in six categories. Each listed test is generally still available from the publisher. Each test entry includes title, author, descriptors (based on terms from the *Thesaurus of ERIC Descriptors*), source of availability, age or grade level, and an abstract. Additional information is included when available, such as the number of test items. The six volumes are: 1. Achievement Tests and Measurement Devices; 2. Vocational Tests and Measurement Devices; 3. Tests for Special Populations; 4. Cognitive Aptitude and Intelligence Tests; 5. Attitude Tests; and 6. Affective Measures and Personality Tests. Subject, author, and title indexes greatly enhance access to these measurement tools. Valuable resource for identifying test materials. Volume 1 was reissued in 1993 with updated information. ETS also maintains a World Wide Web site with its test collection contents.

439.   Keyser, Daniel J., and Sweetland, Richard C., ed. **Test Critiques**. Austin, Tex.: PRO-ED, 1984-1998. 11 vol. $89.00 each vol. 1-9; $92.00 each vol. 10-11. LC: 84-26895. ISBN: 0-89079-596-7 (v. 10). Volumes 1-7 published by Test Corporation of America.

Generally following a standard outline that provides an introduction, practical applications and uses, technical aspects, and a critique of each test, this set of scholarly reviews provides psychometric information related to reliability, validity, and normative development. Focusing on frequently used psychological, educational, and business tests, *Test Critiques* offers valuable information about these tests written by experts in the field. Used in conjunction with its sister publication, *Tests*, the consumer can find complete information about availability and reliability of the major tests used in these areas. A cumulative title index as well as publisher, subject, and author/reviewer indexes provide access to the entire set. Planned as a continuing publication, volume 11, 1998, is the latest published. A valuable source of information about tests.

440. Maddox, Taddy, ed. **Tests: A Comprehensive Reference for Assessments in Psychology, Education and Business**. 4th ed. Austin, Tex.: PRO-ED, 1997. 809 p. $69.00. LC: 96-38299. ISBN: 0-89079-707-2.

Presenting concise descriptions of tests useful to psychologists, educators, and human resources personnel, *Tests* is also helpful to students, librarians, and others seeking information about the broad array of tests available for research and administering. The 4th edition includes several indexes, one of which provides information about publishers of tests not listed in this edition, and another listing tests not included in the 4th edition, but which appeared in the 3rd edition. As a source of information about tests in print and selected information about test publishers not otherwise represented, this is the easiest directory to consult. It does not include evaluative critiques of tests, but those can be found in *Mental Measurements Yearbook* or *Test Critiques*, described elsewhere.

441. Murphy, Linda L., Conoley, Jane Close, and Impara, James C., ed. **Tests in Print IV: An Index to Tests, Test Reviews, and the Literature on Specific Tests**. Lincoln, Nebr.: Buros Institute of Mental Measurements, 1994. 2 vol. $325.00. LC: 83-18866. ISBN: 0-910674-53-1.

Long considered the primary index to test information, *Tests in Print* provides descriptive listings of commercially published tests in print. It also serves as a comprehensive index to the *Mental Measurements Yearbooks* that have been published up to the date of the latest *Tests in Print*. Arranged alphabetically by test title, the 3,009 entries cover 19 different categories of measurement instruments such as achievement, intelligence, and sensory-motor. Supplemental indexes provide test publisher addresses, access by title, acronym, reviewers, authors, subject, and by the area being measured. A critical companion to the *Mental Measurements Yearbooks* and a useful index in its own right.

Guides, Handbooks, and Yearbooks

442.   Keeves, John P., ed. **Educational Research, Methodology, and Measurement: An International Handbook**. 2nd ed. Oxford, Eng.: Pergamon, 1997. 1,054 p. $219.75. LC: 96-52173. ISBN: 0-08-042710-3.

Divided into three major sections, methods of educational inquiry, research methodology, and measurement in educational research, this extremely valuable work provides authoritative articles about aspects of educational research. Many articles have been drawn from the first and second editions of the *International Encyclopedia of Education*. However, new articles have been included as have revisions to earlier entries. For the practitioner, graduate student, or scholar, this is a critical source to key concepts within the area of educational research.

443.   Mertens, Donna M. **Research Methods in Education and Psychology: Integrating Diversity with Quantitative and Qualitative Approaches**. Thousand Oaks, Calif.: Sage, 1998. 422 p. $69.95. LC: 97-4890. ISBN: 0-8039-5827-7.

Written for students at all levels of higher education in the areas of education and psychology, this work offers an introduction to research methods, paradigms, and related issues. From literature reviews to data interpretation to reporting research results, the author provides clear explanations about the research process. Special emphasis is given to ethical issues, the researcher's personal assumptions, and the incorporation of gender and culturally sensitive approaches. Helpful guide to educational research.

444.   **Review of Research in Education**. Washington, D.C.: American Educational Research Association (AERA), 1997. 343 p. LC: 72-89719. ISSN: 0091-732X. ISBN: 0-935302-22-0 (v. 22, 1997).

This annual AERA publication provides reviews of current research in the field of education. Each volume contains thematic segments with chapters addressing differing aspects of those themes. Race and gender, policy issues, and professional development schools are examples of recent topics receiving attention. Also considered are the directions in which educational research is headed and the background for its multidirectional approach. Valuable source for well-researched overviews of education topics.

445.   Schumacher, Dorin. **Get Funded! A Practical Guide for Scholars Seeking Research Support from Business**. Newbury Park, Calif.: Sage, 1992. 288 p. $24.00. LC: 91-32984. ISBN: 0-8039-4440-3.

This guide to soliciting funds from business and industry to support research offers a step-by-step process with clear goals and rationale. After providing an overview of the research and development relationship between industry and academia, the author explains how best to tap into corporate resources. Emphasizing a personal approach, and explaining how to avoid alienating a potential fund provider, the author suggests effective strategies for securing funds and organizing programs. Ethical issues in university-corporate relationships are also covered. A brief bibliography of corporate information sources, a list of references, and an index are included.

446. **Tests in Microfiche**. Princeton, N.J.: Educational Testing Service (ETS), 1975-. annual. $150.00 per set; sets A-X published; $30.00 for cumulative index. ISSN: 0161-2573.

Tests in Microfiche offers the student, researcher, and practitioner the opportunity to view selected unpublished tests to which access may otherwise be very difficult to obtain. Tests may not have had the reliability and validity research that is typical of published tests, but they are still useful as sample research instruments or as models. All types of tests are included and are drawn from the ETS Test Collection. Access is by a separately published print index for each set. A cumulative index covering sets A-X (1975-1998) is available separately from ETS. Terminology used to index each test is from the *Thesaurus of ERIC Descriptors*. Excellent resource for collections that have a demand for reproducible (within copyright limits) test instruments.

447. Walberg, Herbert J., and Haertel, Geneva D., ed. **The International Encyclopedia of Educational Evaluation**. Oxford, Eng.: Pergamon Press, 1990. 796 p. (*Advances in Education*). $157.00. LC: 90-3853. ISBN: 0-08-037269-4. "Based on material from *The International Encyclopedia of Education*, first published 1985, with revisions and updated material."

Although somewhat dated, this handbook provides excellent background information about educational evaluation and measurement. Divided into eight sections, the encyclopedia, which is actually more of a handbook, offers an historical overview of educational evaluation in its preface and a logical sequence of topics in subsequent sections. These sections address: Evaluation Approaches and Strategies, Conduct of Issues in Evaluation Studies, Curriculum Evaluation, Measurement Theory, Measurement Applications, Types of Tests and Examinations, Research Methodology, and Educational Policy and Planning. Supplemented by extensive name and subject indexes, this work is a valuable source of research material related to educational evaluation and measurement.

World Wide Web and Internet Sources

448.   **ERIC/AE Test Locator**. http://www.ericae.net/testcol.htm (accessed February 28, 1999).

The Test Locator is a joint project of ERIC Clearinghouse on Assessment and Evaluation, Educational Testing Service, Buros Institute of Mental Measurements, and Pro-Ed test publishers. It is an excellent resource for identifying information about tests, and is often the best source for identifying obscure references. The database includes not only commonly known tests in all subject areas, but also instruments developed for specific research projects. A companion site offers access to test reviews. The test descriptions are indexed with ERIC thesaurus terms to provide additional access points. Title, author, an abstract, contents, date, and source of availability are indicated for each entry.

Journals

449.   **Alberta Journal of Educational Research**. Vol. 1-. Edmonton, Alberta, Canada: Faculty of Education, University of Alberta, 1955-. quarterly. $45.00 (institutions). ISSN: 0002-4805.

This Canadian-based and focused journal addresses research at all levels of education. It includes brief research reports of studies in progress and has occasional thematic issues. Indexed in: *Canadian Education Index, Current Index to Journals in Education, Educational Administration Abstracts, Multicultural Education Abstracts, Social Sciences Citation Index, Sociology of Education Abstracts.*

450.   **American Educational Research Journal**. Vol. 1-. Washington, D.C.: American Educational Research Association, 1964-. quarterly. $61.00 (institutions). ISSN: 0002-8312.

This AERA publication includes original studies of empirical and theoretical research and educational analyses at all levels of education. Indexed in: *Current Index to Journals in Education, Education Index, Psychological Abstracts, Social Sciences Citation Index.*

451. **Applied Measurement in Education**. Vol. 1-. Mahwah, N.J.: Lawrence Erlbaum, 1988-. quarterly. $295.00 (institutions). ISSN: 0895-7347.

Focuses on research with practical applications to educational testing and measurement. Also available electronically. Indexed in: *Contents Pages in Education, Current Index to Journals in Education, Social Sciences Citation Index.*

452. **Applied Psychological Measurement**. Vol. 1-. Thousand Oaks, Calif.: Sage, 1976-. quarterly. $206.00 (institutions). ISSN: 0146-6216.

Provides empirical research articles within psychological measurement and related disciplines. Also includes brief studies and reports, relevant abstracts of computer programs, and book and software reviews. Indexed in: *Current Index to Journals in Education, Psychological Abstracts, Social Sciences Citation Index.*

453. **Educational and Psychological Measurement**. Vol. 1-. Thousand Oaks, Calif.: Sage Publications, 1941-. 6 issues per year. $298.00 (institutions). ISSN: 0013-1644.

Scholarly articles related to the measurement of individual differences, research reports on the development and use of tests, descriptions of test programs, and practice reports are included in this journal devoted to measurement. Regular features include validity studies, computer program descriptions and reviews, and book reviews. Indexed in: *Current Index to Journals in Education, Education Index, Exceptional Child Education Resources, Higher Education Abstracts, Psychological Abstracts, Social Sciences Citation Index, Special Educational Needs Abstracts.*

454. **Educational Evaluation and Policy Analysis**. Vol. 1-. Washington, D.C.: American Educational Research Association, 1979-. quarterly. $61.00 (institutions). ISSN: 0162-3737.

Containing research articles and brief notes on previously published studies or summaries of studies, this quarterly addresses issues in educational policy analysis and educational evaluation. Theoretical and practical approaches are included. Also includes book reviews. Indexed in: *Current Index to Journals in Education, Education Index, Psychological Abstracts.*

455. **Educational Measurement: Issues and Practice**. Vol. 1-. Washington, D.C.: National Council on Measurement in Education (NCME), 1982-. quarterly. $30.00 (institutions). ISSN: 0731-1745.

NCME news, essay articles, and articles related to practice in testing and measurement form the contents of this journal. The audience includes test specialists, test consumers, and others concerned with issues and practice in measurement. Indexed in: *Current Index to Journals in Education, Education Index, Psychological Abstracts.*

456. **Educational Research**. Vol. 1-. London: Routledge, 1958-. 3 issues per year. $135.00. ISSN: 0013-1881.

Published for the National Foundation for Educational Research in England and Wales (NFER), this journal has an expected focus on educational research in the United Kingdom. Articles include short reports, original research, or discussion pieces in all areas of education. Indexed in: *Current Index to Journals in Education, Education Index, Multicultural Education Abstracts, Psychological Abstracts, Sociology of Education Abstracts.*

457. **Educational Research Quarterly**. Vol. 1-. Grambling, La.: College of Education, Grambling State University, 1950-. quarterly. $120.00 (institutions). ISSN: 0196-5042.

All areas of education at all educational levels are addressed in this research journal. Scholarly articles using a variety of research methodologies are included, as are book reviews, replication studies, and descriptions of research in progress. Measurement and testing topics appear regularly. Indexed in: *Current Index to Journals in Education, Education Index, Psychological Abstracts, Social Sciences Citation Index, Sociology of Education Abstracts, Special Educational Needs Abstracts.*

458. **Educational Researcher**. Vol. 1-. Washington, D.C.: American Educational Research Association (AERA), 1972-. 9 issues per year. $61.00 (institutions). ISSN: 0013-189X.

As the general journal of AERA, received by all members, *Educational Researcher* provides association and conference information, job advertisements, book reviews, and articles that reflect current issues in educational research. All levels and areas of education are addressed. Indexed in: *Current Index to Journals in Education, Education Index, Educational Administration Abstracts, Higher Education Abstracts, Multicultural Education Abstracts, Sociology of Education Abstracts.*

459. **International Journal of Educational Research**. Vol. 1-. Exeter, Eng.: Elsevier Science, 1977-. 14 issues per year in 2 volumes. $755.00 (institutions). ISSN: 0883-0355. Six issues are published

as *Learning and Instruction* in a separate companion volume each year.

Issues are frequently thematic and always have an international focus in this research journal. All aspects of education and its effect on society, economics, and knowledge in general are addressed. Indexed in: *Australian Education Index, Current Index to Journals in Education, Psychological Abstracts, Social Sciences Citation Index.*

460. **International Journal of Qualitative Studies in Education**. Vol. 1-. London: Taylor & Francis, 1988-. quarterly. $398.00 (institutions). ISSN: 0951-8398.

Drawing upon an international authorship, the contents of this publication include both qualitative studies in education and articles about research methodologies in education. Ranging from case studies to ethnographic observations and interviewing, the focus remains research-oriented. Indexed in: *Multicultural Education Abstracts, Sociology of Education Abstracts.*

461. **Journal of Educational and Behavioral Statistics**. Vol. 1-. Washington, D.C.: American Educational Research Association (AERA), 1976-. quarterly. $65.00 (institutions). ISSN: 1076-9986.

Another of the quality AERA publications, this one is published jointly with the American Statistical Association, and focuses on statistical methods and research within the educational and behavioral disciplines. Book reviews and papers with new analytical methods or innovative applications of known techniques are featured. Also included are reviews of current methods and descriptions of lesser known techniques. Indexed in: *Current Index to Journals in Education, Education Index, Psychological Abstracts, Research into Higher Education Abstracts.*

462. **Journal of Educational Measurement**. Vol. 1-. Washington, D.C.: National Council on Measurement in Education, 1964-. quarterly. $50.00 (institutions). ISSN: 0022-0655.

Book reviews and research articles addressing educational measurement, testing, evaluation, and assessment are the focus of this quarterly publication. This is a primary resource for scholarly information about educational testing. Indexed in: *Current Index to Journals in Education, Education Index, Higher Education Abstracts, Psychological Abstracts, Social Sciences Citation Index.*

463. **Journal of Educational Research**. Vol. 1-. Washington, D.C.: Heldref, 1920-. bimonthly. $88.00 (institutions). ISSN: 0022-0671.

Focused on elementary and secondary education, this journal includes research articles and syntheses that address all areas. Experimental, evaluative, ethnographic, and replicative studies are included, as are reviews of methodologies and products. Indexed in: *Current Index to Journals in Education, Education Index, Exceptional Child Education Resources, Multicultural Education Abstracts, Psychological Abstracts, Social Sciences Citation Index.*

464. **Journal of Experimental Education**. Vol. 1-. Washington, D.C.: Heldref, 1932-. quarterly. $75.00 (institutions). ISSN: 0022-0973.

This research-based journal addresses the improvement of educational practice through research, both qualitative and quantitative, at all levels of education and in a wide range of educational settings. Indexed in: *Current Index to Journals in Education, Education Index, Educational Administration Abstracts, Higher Education Abstracts, Multicultural Education Abstracts, Psychological Abstracts, Social Sciences Citation Index.*

465. **Journal of Research and Development in Education**. Vol. 1-. Athens, Ga.: College of Education, University of Georgia, 1967-. quarterly. $25.00 (institutions). ISSN: 0022-426X.

Addressing all areas of education, this journal includes historical studies, experimental and theoretical articles, research reviews, case studies, reports of effective programs, and content analyses. Indexed in: *Current Index to Journals in Education, Education Index, Educational Administration Abstracts, Multicultural Education Abstracts, Psychological Abstracts, Social Sciences Citation Index, Sociology of Education Abstracts.*

466. **Measurement and Evaluation in Counseling and Development**. Vol. 1-. Alexandria, Va.: Association for Assessment in Counseling, a Division of the American Counseling Association, 1968-. quarterly. $50.00 (nonmembers). ISSN: 0748-1756.

As the official journal of the Association for Assessment in Counseling, a strong focus on assessment, measurement, and evaluation within the counseling field is maintained. Research articles range from theoretical to methodologies of interest to measurement specialists, counselors, and administrators in education, industry, or other settings. Indexed in: *Current Index to Journals in Education, Education Index, Higher Education Abstracts, Psychological*

Abstracts, Social Sciences Citation Index, Special Educational Needs Abstracts.

467. **New Directions for Evaluation** . Vol. 1-. San Francisco: Jossey-Bass, 1979-. quarterly. (*Jossey-Bass Education Series*). $115.00 (institutions). ISSN: 1097-6736.

Sponsored by the American Evaluation Association, the contents of this quarterly publication are empirical, methodological, and theoretical articles on evaluation. Program evaluation, specific measurement tools, and social implications of evaluation practices and research are a few of the issues covered in this journal. Each issue is thematic with a separate monographic title. Indexed in: *Current Index to Journals in Education, Education Index, Higher Education Abstracts, Sociological Abstracts.*

468. **Review of Educational Research**. Vol. 1-. Washington, D.C.: American Educational Research Association (AERA), 1931-. quarterly. $61.00 (institutions). ISSN: 0034-6543.

This quality AERA publication provides interpretations and reviews of educational research literature. Methodological issues are addressed as are substantive issues. Educational research in all areas is included. Indexed in: *Current Index to Journals in Education, Education Index, Educational Administration Abstracts, Exceptional Child Education Resources, Higher Education Abstracts, Multicultural Education Abstracts, Psychological Abstracts, Social Sciences Citation Index, Sociology of Education Abstracts, Special Educational Needs Abstracts.*

469. **Scandinavian Journal of Educational Research**. Vol. 1-. Abingdon, Oxfordshire, Eng.: Carfax, 1957-. quarterly. $342.00 (institutions). ISSN: 0031-3831.

International in focus, although emphasizing Scandinavia and the educational innovations occurring there, this research-based journal includes philosophical, historical, comparative, experimental, and survey studies. Indexed in: *British Education Index, Current Index to Journals in Education, Multicultural Education Abstracts, Psychological Abstracts, Sociology of Education Abstracts, Special Educational Needs Abstracts.*

470. **Studies in Educational Evaluation**. Vol. 1-. Exeter, Eng.: Elsevier Science, 1974-. quarterly. $437.00 (institutions). ISSN: 0191-491X.

Educational evaluation studies from around the world are presented in this research journal. Discussion of evaluation methods, program evaluations, student assessments, and reviews of books and evaluation studies are included. Indexed in: *Current Index to Journals in Education, Education Index, Higher Education Abstracts, Multicultural Education Abstracts.*

14

EDUCATIONAL PSYCHOLOGY

Dictionaries and Encyclopedias

471. De Corte, Erik, and Weinert, Franz E., ed. **International Encyclopedia of Developmental and Instructional Psychology**. Oxford, Eng.: Elsevier Science, 1996. 882 p. $219.75. LC: 96-17900. ISBN: 0-08-042980-7.

   Drawing together the links between developmental and instructional psychology, the editors have developed a framework for presenting articles in 17 different categories. These categories address the history of developmental and instructional psychology, general issues, cultural concepts, developmental stages, biological approaches, personality development, cognitive development, learning theories and models, processes and outcomes, curriculum, aspects of learning, individual differences, learning environment, technology and learning, adult learning, special needs, and assessment. The articles in each of these categories are new or updated from the second edition of the *International Encyclopedia of Education*. Extensive name and subject indexes provide access to particular aspects of these two intertwined areas.

472. Fagan, Thomas K., and Warden, Paul G., ed. **Historical Encyclopedia of School Psychology**. Westport, Conn.: Greenwood Press, 1996. 448 p. $99.50. LC: 95-23614. ISBN: 0-313-29015-6.

   As much a dictionary as an encyclopedia, each entry in this work includes a definition or description of a term, followed by its historical context where applicable, and a few key references to related works. The entries include major figures in the field who are deceased, events, places, concepts, and practices in the field of school psychology. A clear distinction is made between school psychology, considered a professional practice specialty within psychology, and educational psychology, a research-oriented field dealing with the problems of education and learning. References to related terms appear within most entries, and the index includes not only the main entry for each term, but also relevant related entries. An appendix includes sources for further information, such as organizations, journals, major books, a list of contemporary figures in the field, and a brief bibliography of historical sources about school psychology. Useful, specialized resource.

Guides, Handbooks, and Yearbooks

473. Berliner, David C., and Calfee, Robert C., ed. **Handbook of Educational Psychology**. New York: Simon & Schuster Macmillan, 1996. 1,071 p. $75.00. LC: 95-43348. ISBN: 0-02-897089-6.

Developed as a project of the Division of Educational Psychology of the American Psychological Association, this handbook emphasizes cognition as the theoretical framework for the practice of educational psychology. Each of the 33 chapters falls into the following headings: cognition and motivation; development and individual differences; school curriculum and psychology; teaching and instruction; and, foundations of the discipline. Directed to graduate students, university educators, and researchers, the text includes extensive references, a name index, and a thorough subject index.

474. Reynolds, Cecil R., and Gutkin, Terry B., ed. **Handbook of School Psychology**. 3rd ed. New York: John Wiley & Sons, 1999. 1,200 p. $101.50. LC: 98-17618. ISBN: 0-471-12205-X.

The third edition of this handbook brings together a series of new and updated chapters that offer both current scientific information and practical advice in school psychology. Addressed in five sections are the history and current state of school psychology; school psychology and the study of behavior; psychological and educational assessment; interventions focusing on children; and, interventions focusing on support systems. Each chapter is supplemented by references. Includes extensive author and subject indexes.

Journals

475. **Cognition and Instruction**. Vol. 1-. Mahwah, N.J.: Lawrence Erlbaum, 1983-. quarterly. $225.00. ISSN: 0737-0008.

This heavily research-based journal provides peer-reviewed articles that address cognitive evaluation of instructional activities and interventions. Also available electronically. Indexed in: *Current Index to Journals in Education, Psychological Abstracts, Social Sciences Citation Index.*

476. **Contemporary Educational Psychology**. Vol. 1-. Orlando, Fla.: Academic Press, 1976-. quarterly. $275.00 (institutions). ISSN: 0361-476X.

Research articles, brief research reports, and research agenda articles comprise the contents of this refereed journal. All levels of education are included as they relate to psychological theory and practice in the educational setting. Also available electronically. Indexed in: *Current Index to Journals in Education.*

477. **Educational Psychologist**. Vol. 1-. Mahwah, N.J.: Lawrence Erlbaum, 1963-. quarterly. $270.00 (institutions). ISSN: 0046-1520.

Scholarly essays, reviews, and theoretical and conceptual articles that relate to educational psychology are included in this publication. *Educational Psychologist* is part of the membership privileges of the Division of Educational Psychology of the American Psychological Association. Thematic issues are also published. Indexed in: *Psychological Abstracts, Social Sciences Citation Index.*

478. **Educational Psychology: An International Journal of Experimental Educational Psychology**. Vol. 1-. Abingdon, Oxfordshire, Eng.: Carfax, 1981-. quarterly. $604.00 (institutions). ISSN: 0144-3410.

Emphasizing applied research to educational psychology issues in preschool through higher education, as well as to special needs populations, this internationally focused journal gives extra attention to experimental studies. Also includes book reviews. Indexed in: *Current Index to Journals in Education, Multicultural Education Abstracts, Psychological Abstracts, Sociology of Education Abstracts, Special Educational Needs Abstracts.*

479.   **Educational Psychology Review**. Vol. 1-. New York: Plenum, 1989-. quarterly. $215.00 (institutions). ISSN: 1040-726X.

   International in focus, this journal incorporates review articles in educational psychology that address several key areas such as measurement, cognition, individual differences, and counseling. Commentaries and special thematic issues are also featured periodically. Indexed in: *Education Index, Multicultural Education Abstracts, Psychological Abstracts, Sociology of Education Abstracts, Special Educational Needs Abstracts.*

480.   **Instructional Science: An International Journal of Learning and Cognition**. Vol. 1-. Dordrecht, The Netherlands: Kluwer Academic, 1971-. bimonthly. $357.50 . ISSN: 0020-4277.

   Scholarly articles addressing the theory and practice of learning and the instructional process comprise the contents of this journal. International in focus, the articles address a wide range of topics within the areas of learning and cognition. Indexed in: *Education Index, Higher Education Abstracts, Multicultural Education Abstracts, Psychological Abstracts, Social Sciences Citation Index, Sociology of Education Abstracts.*

481.   **Journal of Counseling and Development**. Vol.1-. Alexandria, Va.: American Counseling Association (ACA), 1922-. 6 issues per year. $97.00 (institutions). ISSN: 0748-9633.

   Formerly *Personnel and Guidance Journal*, this publication offers information and research of interest to counselors, counseling psychologists, and student personnel specialists at all levels of education. Relevant topics are addressed in research articles, historical overviews, reports of innovative practices and programs, assessment and diagnosis columns, and literature reviews. Indexed in: *Current Index to Journals in Education, Education Index, Educational Administration Abstracts, Exceptional Child Education Resources, Higher Education Abstracts, Psychological Abstracts, Social Sciences Citation Index.*

482.   **Journal of Educational Psychology**. Vol. 1-. Washington, D.C.: American Psychological Association, 1910-. quarterly. $194.00 (institutions). ISSN: 0022-0663.

   Every level of education is addressed in the contents of the psychological research articles dealing with cognition, motivation, special populations, learning styles and more presented in this publication. Occasional theoretical and review articles are also included. Indexed in: *Current Index to Journals in Education, Education Index, Exceptional Child Education Resources, Higher*

Education Abstracts, Multicultural Education Abstracts, Psychological Abstracts, Social Sciences Citation Index.

483. **Journal of the Learning Sciences**. Vol. 1-. Mahwah, N.J.: Lawrence Erlbaum, 1991-. quarterly. $280.00 (institutions). ISSN: 1050-8406.

Focusing on the cognitive sciences, this journal presents research articles on learning, educational psychology, educational technology, and artificial intelligence. Book reviews are included. Indexed in: *Current Index to Journals in Education, Multicultural Education Abstracts, Psychological Abstracts, Social Sciences Citation Index.*

484. **Learning and Individual Differences: A Multidisciplinary Journal in Education**. Vol. 1-. Stamford, Conn.: JAI Press, 1989-. quarterly. $205.00 (institutions). ISSN: 1041-6080.

Research and theoretical articles, commentaries, and reports of applications of methods are included in this multidisciplinary journal. Topics addressed include memory, cognition, intelligence, motivation, development, reading, and testing. Indexed in: *Education Index, Psychological Abstracts, Social Sciences Citation Index.*

485. **Learning and Motivation**. Vol. 1-. Orlando, Fla.: Academic Press, 1970-. quarterly. $365.00 (institutions). ISSN: 0023-9690.

With a strong emphasis on experimental psychological research, this journal addresses learning and motivation in its mechanisms and processes. Biological and evolutionary influences are considered. Suitable for an education collection with a strong emphasis on psychological research. Also available electronically. Indexed in: *Psychological Abstracts, Social Sciences Citation Index.*

486. **Merrill-Palmer Quarterly: Journal of Developmental Psychology**. Vol. 1-. Detroit, Mich.: Wayne State University Press, 1954-. quarterly. $86.00 (institutions). ISSN: 0272-930X.

Despite its strong focus on developmental psychology, this journal includes relevant research articles and book reviews on child development within the context of the school. Valuable resource for infant, child, and adolescent development research. Indexed in: *Current Index to Journals in Education, Education Index, Exceptional Child Education Resources, Multicultural Education Abstracts, Psychological Abstracts, Social Sciences Citation Index, Sociology of Education Abstracts, Special Educational Needs Abstracts.*

487.   **Psychology in the Schools**. Vol. 1-. New York: John Wiley & Sons, 1964-. bimonthly. $224.00 (institutions). ISSN: 0033-3085.

Aimed not only at schools, but also colleges and other organizations where educational psychologists, teachers, counselors, administrators, and other personnel workers deal with issues related to evaluation and assessment, this journal provides a practice-oriented forum. Research, opinion, and practice articles are included, as are book and test reviews. Indexed in: *Current Index to Journals in Education, Education Index, Exceptional Child Education Resources, Multicultural Education Abstracts, Psychological Abstracts, Social Sciences Citation Index, Special Educational Needs Abstracts.*

488.   **School Psychology Review**. Vol. 1-. Bethesda, Md.: National Association of School Psychologists, 1972-. quarterly. $80.00 (institutions). ISSN: 0279-6015.

Scholarly articles on research, training, and practice in school psychology are the focus of this association-published journal. Case studies, theoretical and applied research articles, descriptions of intervention techniques, and occasional reviews of books, tests, and related materials are included. Segments of two or three issues each year are devoted to thematic topics. Also available electronically. Indexed in: *Current Index to Journals in Education, Education Index, Psychological Abstracts, Social Sciences Citation Index.*

AUTHOR INDEX

Accardo, Pasquale J. 268
Aldrich, Richard 111, 112
Alkin, Marvin C. 436
Altbach, Philip G. 165
Anaya, Alison 170
Anderegg, M. L. 270
Andersen, Charles J. 208
Anderson, Beth 16
Anderson, Lorin W. 2
Atwell, Robert H. 171

Baker, Colin 248
Banks, Cherry A. McGee 251
Banks, James A. 251
Barr, Rebecca 365
Barrow, Robin 3
Bauer, David G. 172
Berger, James L. 119
Berliner, David C. 473
Bernhard, Judith 149
Berry, Dorothea M. 25
Biddle, Bruce J. 26
Birch, Jack W. 203
Blair, Judy 325
Blake, David 4
Bowman, J. Wilson 173
Branch, Robert Maribe 120
Brandt, Ronald S. 10
British Council, National Academic Rec-
     ognition Information Centre for
     the United Kingdom (NARIC)
     192
Brown, David 27, 360
Brown, Neil L. 250
Buchanan, Mary 275
Buchanan, Michelle 275
Burgess, William E. 311
Butler, Gregory S. 18
Buttery, Thomas J. 42

Cabell, David W. E. 19
Calfee, Robert C. 473
Caspard, Pierre 425
Chambliss, J. J. 423
Clark, Burton R. 166
Clarke, Peter B. 28
Clayton, Irene A. 367
Colangelo, Nicholas 276
Colby, Anita Y. 12
College Entrance Examination Board 195
Compton, Carolyn 277
Conoley, Jane Close 437, 441
Council for Exceptional Children 278
Cullen, Patrick 176
Cummings, William K. 29

Danesy, Frank C. 196
Davis, Gary A. 276
Davis, Lynne 211
Davis, Todd M. 345
De Corte, Erik 471
Dejnozka, Edward L. 5
Devine, Mary Elizabeth 204
Doughty, Harold R. 175
Drozdowski, Mark J. 176

Edwards, Alan F., Jr. 177
Ellington, Henry 116
Entwistle, Noel 30

Fagan, Thomas K. 472
Farrell, Michael 31
Firth, Gerald R. 411
Fisher, Millard T. 150
Fiske, Edward B. 178

Fitzgerald, Mary Ann 120
Fitzpatrick, Jacqueline 197
Flattau, Pamela Ebert 209
Frazier, Gloria G. 137
Freed, Melvyn N. 32
Fromberg, Doris Pronin 136
Fullan, Michael 34

Gabel, Dorothy L. 363
Goldberger, Marvin L. 209
Good, Thomas L. 26
Goodson, Ivor F. 26
Gordon, Peter 9, 111, 112
Gough, Jeanne 33
Gourman, Jack 198, 199
Guidry, Josee G. 325
Gutek, Gerald L. 435
Gutkin, Terry B. 474
Guyton, Edith 42

Haertel, Geneva D. 447
Halstead, Kent 55
Hanley, Vincent 4
Hargreaves, Andy 34
Harris, Duncan 116
Hattendorf Westney, Lynn C. 56
Heller, Kurt A. 280
Hess, Robert K. 32
Holmes, Patricia A. 35
Hopkins, David 34
Houston, James E. 6, 7
Husen, Torsten 8

Impara, James C. 437, 441

Jarvis, Peter 309
Jonassen, David H. 122
Jones, Sylvia Prys 248
Jones-Wilson, Faustine C. 249

Kamil, Michael L. 365
Kapel, David E. 5
Kaplin, William A. 201
Keeves, John P. 442
Kerry, Carolle 31
Kerry, Trevor 31
Keyser, Daniel J. 439

Klein, Barry 36
Knowles, Asa S. 167
Koeppe, Richard P. 14
Kurian, George Thomas 338

Lawton, Denis 9
Lee, Barbara A. 201
Leibee, Howard C. 367
Leider, Anna J. 202
Lewy, Arieh 356
Lieberman, Ann 34
Logue, Robert 178
Loke, Wing Hong 37

Mackenzie, Leslie 23
Maddox, Taddy 440
Maher, Brendan A. 209
Mann, Lester 269
Mastain, Richard K. 39
Mauch, James E. 203
McBrien, J. Lynn 10
McGinn, Noel F. 29
McManama, Jerre L. 367
Mertens, Donna M. 443
Messersmith, Lloyd L. 367
Milburn, Geoffrey 3
Miller, Elizabeth B. 359
Mintz, Jerry 315
Mitchell, Bruce M. 252
Mitchell, Robert 180
Monks, Franz J. 280
Mosenthal, Peter 365
Murphy, Linda L. 441

National Society for the Study of Educa-
    tion 40
Neave, Guy 166
Nehmer, Kathleen Suttles 123, 145
Nettles, Michael T. 253
Nicolescu, Adrian 168
Noble, Keith Allan 11

Ohles, Frederik 113
Ohles, John F. 114
Ohles, Shirley M. 113

Pajak, Edward F.   411
Palmer, James C.   12
Passow, A. Harry   280
Patt, Carol A.   7
Pearson, P. David   365
Perna, Laura W.   253
Perry, Phyllis J.   366
Peltzman, Barbara Ruth   163
Phillipe, Kent A.   210
Pierce, David   171
Postlethwaite, T. Neville   8, 339
Price, Jerry D.   125
Prochner, Lawrence   149

Raffel, Jeffrey A.   424
Rahn, Mikala L.   35
Ramsay, John G.   113
Reynolds, Cecil R.   269, 474
Reynolds, Maynard C.   281
Rich, Elizabeth H.   143, 186
Rider, Betty L.   124
Robin, Bernard   125
Rodenhouse, Mary Pat   187
Ryan, Joseph M.   32

Saha, Lawrence J.   13
Salsbury, Robert E.   252
Schlachter, Gail Ann   188
Schmottlach, Neil   367
Schumacher, Dorin   445
Seaton, Don Cash   367
Secrist, Jan   197
Shafritz, Jay M.   14
Shaver, James P.   369
Sheffield, Phil   51
Shokraii, Nina H.   146
Sickles, Robert N.   137
Sikula, John   42
Silvey, Marvin W.   24
Silvey, Merrill H.   24
Slack, James D.   18
Solomon, Raymond   315
Solomon, Sidney   315
Soper, Elizabeth W.   14
Sparks, Linda   164

Spodek, Bernard   147
Steen, Sara J.   342
Sullivan, Eugene   314
Summerfield, Carol   204
Sweetland, Richard C.   439

Thorson, Marcie Kisner   316
Thrasher, Michele   412
Touchton, Judith G.   211
Tryneski, John   148
Tuijnman, Albert C.   310

U.S. Department of Education. National
   Center for Education Statistics
   58, 59
Unger, Harlow G.   15

Vergason, Glenn A.   270
Vuturo, Christopher   189

Walberg, Herbert J.   281, 447
Wang, Margaret C.   281
Warden, Paul G.   472
Washburn, David E.   250
Weber, R. David   188
Weinert, Franz E.   471
Weller, Carol   275
Weller, Carolyn R.   7
Whitman, Barbara Y.   268
Wickremasinghe, Walter   344
Williams, Leslie R.   136
Williams, Phillip   271
Willis, Dee Anna   125
Willis, Jerry   125
Wood, Donna   190
Woodill, Gary A.   149
Wright, Debra J.   197
Wright, Philip C.   325

Youssef, Sarah E.   146

TITLE INDEX

Titles appearing with an asterisk (*) refer to former titles or other title information appearing in the annotation or notes for that entry.

AAESPH Review* 300
The A's and B's of Academic Scholarships 202
Academe: Bulletin of the American Association of University Professors 214
Academic Therapy* 293
Academic Year Abroad 1998/99 342
Accredited Institutions of Postsecondary Education, Programs, Candidates 1996-97 170
Adult Education Quarterly: A Journal of Research and Theory in Adult Education 318
The Adult Learner's Guide to Alternative and External Degree Programs 314
Adult Learning 319
Advisory List of International Educational Travel and Exchange Programs, 1996-97 340
African American Education Data Book 253
Alberta Journal of Educational Research 449
Almanac of Higher Education 1995 207
America's Black and Tribal Colleges 173
American Biology Teacher 375
American Community Colleges: A Guide 171
American Community, Technical, and Junior Colleges: A Guide* 171
American Educational Research Journal 450
American Educator 69
American Educator's Encyclopedia 5
American Journal of Distance Education 320

American Journal of Education 70
American School Board Journal 71
American School Directory (ASD) 60
American School & University 72
American Universities and Colleges 169
Annual Register of Grant Support: A Directory of Funding Sources 1999 17
Applied Measurement in Education 451
Applied Psychological Measurement 452
Art Education 376
Australian Education Index 43
AV Communication Review* 127

Behavioral Disorders 284
Bibliographic Guide to Education 1
A Bibliographic Guide to Educational Research 25
Bilingual Research Journal 255
Biographical Dictionary of American Educators 114
Biographical Dictionary of Modern American Educators 113
Biographical Dictionary of North American and European Educationists 112
Black Issues in Higher Education 215
Blackwell Handbook of Education 31
Blue Web'n: A Library of Blue Ribbon Learning Sites on the Web 372
British Education Index 51
British Journal of Educational Studies 73
British Journal of Educational Technology 126
British Journal of Guidance and Counselling 327

British Journal of Sociology of Education 74

British Journal of Special Education 285

British Journal of Teacher Education* 92

Bunting and Lyon Blue Book* 142

Business Education Forum 328

Business Education Index 370

Cabell's Directory of Publishing Opportunities in Education 19

Campus-Free College Degrees 316

Canadian Education Index/Repertoire Canadien Sur l'Education 44

Canadian Journal of Education/Revue Canadienne de l'education 75

Career Development for Exceptional Individuals 286

Career Development Quarterly 329

Change: The Magazine of Higher Learning 216

Chicorel Abstracts on Reading and Learning Disabilities* 395

Childhood Education: Infancy Through Early Adolescence 151

Chinese Educational Resources Information Centre Project (Chinese ERIC) 61

Chinese ERIC* 61

Chronicle of Higher Education 217

A Classification of Institutions of Higher Education 193

Clearing House 152

Cognition and Instruction 475

College and University 218

College and University Home Pages 212

College and University Rankings 213

College Blue Book 174

College Board Review 219

College Catalog Collections on Microfiche 194

College Explorer* 195

College Handbook 1999 195

College Student Journal: A Journal Pertaining to College Students and Post-Secondary Instruction 220

College Student Personnel Abstracts* 205

College Teaching 221

Commonwealth Universities Yearbook. A Directory to the Universities of the Commonwealth and the Handbook of Their Associations 20

Communication Education 377

Community College Journal 222

Community College Journal of Research and Practice 223

Community College Review 224

Comparative Education 349

Comparative Education Review 350

Comparative Guide to American Elementary & Secondary Schools 144

Compare: A Journal of Comparative Education 351

The Complete Grants Sourcebook for Higher Education 172

Complete Learning Disabilities Directory, 1998/99 272

The Condition of Education 59

Condition of Teaching: A State-by-State Analysis, 1990 54

Contemporary Education 76

Contemporary Educational Psychology 476

Contents Pages in Education 45

Continuing Higher Education Review 225

Convergence 321

Council on Technology Teacher Education Yearbook * 124

Counselor Education and Supervision 330

Country Teacher* 101

A Critical Dictionary of Educational Concepts: An Appraisal of Selected Ideas and Issues in Educational Theory and Practice 3

Cultural Foundations of Education: A Biographical Introduction 435

CUPA Journal 226

Current Index to Journals in Education (CIJE) 46

Curriculum Inquiry 378

Curriculum Review: A Monthly Report on What Works in Our Schools 379

Curriculum Theory Network* 378

Day Care and Early Education* 154

Developing Educational Standards 62

Dictionary of British Educationists 111
Dictionary of Developmental Disabilities
    Terminology 268
Dictionary of Education 9
Dictionary of Educational Acronyms,
    Abbreviations, and Initialisms 12
The Dictionary of Educational Terms 4
Dictionary of Instructional Technology
    116
Dictionary of Special Education and Reha-
    bilitation 270
Digest of Education Statistics 58
Dimensions of Early Childhood 153
Directory for Exceptional Children: A
    Listing of Educational and Train-
    ing Facilities 1994-95 273
Directory of College Facilities and
    Services for People with Disabili-
    ties 274
Directory of Curriculum Materials Cen-
    ters 16
Directory of Financial Aids for Minori-
    ties* 188
Directory of Innovations in High Schools
    137
Directory of Public School Systems in the
    United States 1997-98 21
Directory of State Education Agencies
    22
Diversity in Technology Education 124

Early Childhood Education Journal 154
Early Childhood Research Quarterly 155
Early Education and Development 156
Early Years* 108
Economics of Education Review 414
Education 77
Education and Society: International Jour-
    nal in Education and Sociology
    352
Education and Training in Mental Retarda-
    tion and Developmental Disabili-
    ties 287
Education at a Glance: OECD Indicators
    1997 346
Education Digest 78
Education Index 47
Education Laws: A Compilation of Stat-
    utes in Effect Today 412
Education Sourcebook 33
Education Virtual Library 63

Education Week 79
Educational Administration Abstracts 413
Educational Administration Quarterly
    415
Educational and Psychological Measure-
    ment 453
Educational Communication and Technol-
    ogy Journal* 127
Educational Evaluation and Policy Analy-
    sis 454
Educational Forum 80
Educational Horizons 81
Educational Information Resources Infor-
    mation Center: ERIC 64
Educational Leadership 82
Educational Measurement: Issues and
    Practice 455
Educational Media and Technology Year-
    book 120
Educational Opportunity Guide: A Direc-
    tory of Programs for the Gifted
    279
Educational Philosophy and Theory 428
Educational Policy 83
Educational Psychologist 477
Educational Psychology: An International
    Journal of Experimental Educa-
    tional Psychology 478
Educational Psychology Review 479
Educational Rankings Annual 1999 56
Educational Research 456
Educational Research, Methodology, and
    Measurement: An International
    Handbook 442
Educational Research Quarterly 457
Educational Researcher 458
Educational Studies 84
Educational Studies: A Journal in the
    Foundations of Education 429
Educational Technology Research and De-
    velopment 127
Educational Technology: The Magazine
    for Managers of Change in Educa-
    tion 128
Educational Theory 430
Educator's Desk Reference (EDR): A
    Sourcebook of Educational Infor-
    mation and Research 32
Educators Guide to Free Films, Filmstrips
    and Slides 121
Educators Guide to Free Guidance Materi-
    als 326

Educators Guide to Free Science Materials 361
Educators Guide to Free Social Studies Materials 362
Educators Guide to Free Videotapes 119
Educators Index of Free Materials* 368
Educators Resource Directory* 23
El-Hi Textbooks and Serials in Print 1998 357
Elementary English* 393
Elementary School Journal 157
Elementary Teachers Guide to Free Curriculum Materials 1998-1999 145
ELT Journal 256
Encyclopedia of African-American Education 249
Encyclopedia of American Education 15
Encyclopedia of Bilingualism and Bilingual Education 248
Encyclopedia of Early Childhood Education 136
Encyclopedia of Education Information, 1997 23
Encyclopedia of Educational Research 436
Encyclopedia of Higher Education 166
Encyclopedia of Special Education: A Reference for the Education of the Handicapped and Other Exceptional Children and Adults 269
English Education: Official Journal of the Conference on English Education 380
English for Specific Purposes 257
English Journal 381
Equity and Excellence in Education 258
ERIC/AE Test Locator 448
ERIC Identifier Authority List (IAL) 7
EROD: Education Resource Organizations Directory 65
ESP Journal* 257
ETS Test Collection Catalog 438
European Education: A Journal of Translations 353
European Journal of Education: Research, Development and Policies 354
Exceptional Child* 292
Exceptional Child Education Resources 282

Exceptional Children 288
Exceptionality 289

Fact Book on Higher Education 1997 208
Fact Book on Women in Higher Education 211
The Facts on File Dictionary of Education 14
Financial Aid for Native Americans, 1997-1999 188
Finding Out in Education: A Guide to Sources of Information 28
Fiske Guide to Colleges 1999 178
For the Learning of Mathematics: An International Journal of Mathematics Education 382

GEM: The Gateway to Educational Materials 373
Gender and Education 85
Get Funded! A Practical Guide for Scholars Seeking Research Support from Business 445
Gifted Child Quarterly 290
Gifted Education International 291
Goldmine, 1995-96: Finding Free and Low-Cost Resources for Teaching 360
The Gourman Report: A Rating of Graduate and Professional Programs in American and International Universities 198
The Gourman Report: A Rating of Undergraduate Programs in American and International Universities 199
A Guide to 100 Tests for Special Education 277
Guide to American Educational Directories 36
Guide to American Graduate Schools 175
Guide to Free Computer Materials 123
A Guide to Journals in Psychology and Education 37
Guide to Math Materials: Resources to Support the NCTM Standards 366
Guide to the Successful Thesis and Dissertation: A Handbook for Students and Faculty 203

Guidebook of Federal Resources for K-12 Mathematics and Science 358

Handbook of Alternative Education 315
Handbook of Educational Ideas and Practices 30
Handbook of Educational Psychology 473
Handbook of Gifted Education 276
The Handbook of Private Schools: An Annual Descriptive Survey of Independent Education 138
Handbook of Reading Research 365
Handbook of Research for Educational Communications and Technology 122
Handbook of Research on Multicultural Education 251
Handbook of Research on School Supervision 411
Handbook of Research on Science Teaching and Learning 363
Handbook of Research on Social Studies Teaching and Learning 369
Handbook of Research on Teacher Education 42
Handbook of Research on the Education of Young Children 147
Handbook of School Psychology 474
Handbook of Special and Remedial Education: Research and Practice 281
Handbook of World Education: A Comparative Guide to Higher Education and Educational Systems of the World 344
Harvard Educational Review 86
Harvard Teachers Record* 86
HEP . . . Higher Education Directory 187
High School Journal 158
High School Magazine for Principals, Assistant Principals, and All High School Leaders 416
Higher Education Abstracts 205
Higher Education Credentials: A Guide to Educational Systems in Europe and North America 196
Higher Education Directory* 187
Higher Education Quarterly 227
Higher Education: The International Journal of Higher Education and Educational Planning 228

Historical Dictionary of School Segregation and Desegregation: The American Experience 424
Historical Encyclopedia of School Psychology 472
History of Education 431
History of Education Museums and Collections International Directory 426
History of Education Quarterly 432
History of Education Site 427
History Teacher 383

Independent School 159
Independent Study Catalog 312
Index of Majors and Graduate Degrees 1999 200
Index to Selected British Educational Periodicals* 51
Information Sources for Teachers 27
Initiatives 87
Innovations in Education and Training International 229
Innovative Higher Education 230
Insider's Guide to Graduate Programs in Education 176
Institutions of Higher Education: An International Bibliography 164
Instructional Innovator* 135
Instructional Science: An International Journal of Learning and Cognition 480
Instructor 88
Integrateducation* 258
Interchange: A Quarterly Review of Education 89
Interdisciplinary Undergraduate Programs: A Directory 177
International Bulletin of Bibliography on Education 48
An International Dictionary of Adult and Continuing Education 309
International Dictionary of University Histories 204
International Education Quotations Encyclopaedia 11
International Encyclopedia of Adult Education and Training 310
The International Encyclopedia of Curriculum 356

International Encyclopedia of Developmental and Instructional Psychology 471
The International Encyclopedia of Education 8
The International Encyclopedia of Educational Evaluation 447
International Encyclopedia of Higher Education 167
International Encyclopedia of National Systems of Education 339
International Encyclopedia of Teaching and Teacher Education 2
International Encyclopedia of the Sociology of Education 13
International Guide for Research in the History of Education 425
International Guide to Qualifications in Education 192
International Handbook of Early Childhood Education 149
International Handbook of Education and Development: Preparing Schools, Students and Nations for the Twenty-First Century 29
International Handbook of Educational Change 34
International Handbook of Research and Development of Giftedness and Talent 280
International Handbook of Teachers and Teaching 26
International Handbook of Universities 179
International Higher Education: An Encyclopedia 165
International Journal of Disability, Development and Education 292
International Journal of Educational Development 355
International Journal of Educational Research 459
International Journal of Qualitative Studies in Education 460
International Journal of Science Education 384
International Review of Education 90
International Study Telecom Directory 341
Internet Resource Directory for K-12 Teachers and Librarians 359
Intervention in School and Clinic 293

IRAL: International Review of Applied Linguistics in Language Teaching 259

JEM* 462
Journal for Research in Mathematics Education 385
Journal for the Education of the Gifted 294
Journal of Adolescent & Adult Literacy 386
Journal of Aesthetic Education 387
Journal of Agricultural Education 331
Journal of Alcohol and Drug Education 388
Journal of Blacks in Higher Education 231
Journal of Career Development 332
Journal of College and University Law 232
Journal of College Student Development 233
Journal of College Student Personnel* 233
Journal of Computers in Mathematics and Science Teaching 129
Journal of Continuing Higher Education 322
Journal of Cooperative Education 333
Journal of Counseling and Development 481
Journal of Curriculum and Supervision 389
Journal of Curriculum Studies 390
Journal of Developmental and Remedial Education* 295
Journal of Developmental Education 295
Journal of Developmental Reading* 386
Journal of Early Intervention 296
Journal of Education 91
Journal of Education Finance 417
Journal of Education for Students Placed at Risk 297
Journal of Education for Teaching 92
Journal of Educational Administration 418
Journal of Educational and Behavioral Statistics 461
Journal of Educational Measurement 462
Journal of Educational Psychology 482
Journal of Educational Research 463

Journal of Experiential Education   391
Journal of Experimental Education   464
Journal of General Education   93
Journal of Higher Education   234
Journal of Industrial Teacher Education   334
Journal of Instructional Development*   127
Journal of Learning Disabilities   298
Journal of Multilingual and Multicultural Development   260
Journal of Negro Education   261
Journal of Reading*   386
Journal of Reading, Writing, and Learning Disabilities International*   395
Journal of Research and Development in Education   465
Journal of Research in Childhood Education: An International Journal of Research on the Education of Children, Infancy Through Early Adolescence   160
Journal of Research in Science Teaching   392
Journal of Research on Computing in Education   130
Journal of Special Education   299
Journal of Teacher Education   94
Journal of Technology Education   131
Journal of the American Association of Teacher Educators in Agriculture*   331
Journal of the Association for Persons with Severe Handicaps   300
Journal of the Division for Early Childhood*   296
Journal of the Learning Sciences   483
Journal of Vocational Behavior   335
Journal of Vocational Education and Training   336
Journal of Vocational Education Research   337

Language and Language Behavior Abstracts*   49
Language Arts   393
Language Learning: A Journal of Research in Language Studies   262
The Language of Learning: A Guide to Education Terms   10

The Latest and Best of TESS: The Educational Software Selector   117
The Law of Higher Education: A Comprehensive Guide to Legal Implications of Administrative Decision Making   201
Learning*   96
Learning and Individual Differences: A Multidisciplinary Journal in Education   484
Learning and Instruction: The Journal of the European Association for Research on Learning and Instruction   95
Learning and Motivation   485
Learning Disability Quarterly   301
Learning Page: American Memory   374
Liberal Education   235
Linguistics and Language Behavior Abstracts   49
LLBA*   49

Mailbox Teacher   96
Making Standards Matter: An Annual Fifty-State Report on Efforts to Raise Academic Standards   38
Man-Society-Technology*   134
Master's Theses Directories   24
Master's Theses in Education*   24
Measurement and Evaluation in Counseling and Development   466
Mental Measurements Yearbook   437
Mental Retardation   302
Merrill-Palmer Quarterly: Journal of Developmental Psychology   486
Middle School Journal   161
Montessori Life   394
Multicultural Education   263
Multicultural Education: An International Guide to Research, Policies and Programs   252
The Multicultural Education Directory   250
Multicultural Student's Guide to Colleges: What Every African-American, Asian-American, Hispanic and Native American Applicant Needs to Know About America's Top Schools   180
Multilingual Lexicon of Higher Education   168

NACADA Journal: The Journal of the National Academic Advising Association 236

NASDTEC Manual 1991: Manual on Certification and Preparation of Educational Personnel in the United States 39

NASPA Journal 237

NASSP Bulletin 419

National Assessment of Educational Progress 66

National Faculty Directory 1999 181

National Guide to Funding for Elementary and Secondary Education 143

National Guide to Funding in Higher Education 186

National Profile of Community Colleges: Trends and Statistics 1997-1998 210

National Public School Locator 67

National Standard for Civics and Government 364

NCBE Web Site 254

NCEA/Ganley's Catholic Schools in America 150

NEA Almanac of Higher Education 182

NEA Handbook 41

New Directions for Adult and Continuing Education 323

New Directions for Community Colleges 238

New Directions for Evaluation 467

New Directions for Higher Education 239

New Directions for Institutional Research 240

New Directions for Student Services 241

New Directions for Teaching and Learning 242

Only the Best: The Annual Guide to the Highest-Rated Educational Software and Multimedia 118

Open Doors: Report on International Educational Exchange 1996/1997 345

Open Learning 324

Opportunities for Vocational Study: A Directory of Learning Programs Sponsored by North American Non-Profit Associations 325

Oryx Guide to Distance Learning: A Comprehensive Listing of Electronic and Other Media-Assisted Courses 311

Paedagogica Historica: International Journal of the History of Education 433

Patterson's American Education 1997 139

Patterson's Elementary Education 1997 140

Peabody Journal of Education 97

Personnel and Guidance Journal* 481

Peterson's Annual Guides to Graduate Study 183

Peterson's Distance Learning 1997 313

Peterson's Internships 1999 184

Peterson's Private Secondary Schools, 1997-98 141

Peterson's Register of Higher Education 185

Phi Delta Kappan 98

Philosophy of Education: An Encyclopedia 423

Physical Education Handbook 367

Physical Education Index 371

Pioneers of Early Childhood Education: A Bio-Bibliographical Guide 163

Planning for Higher Education 243

Principal 420

Private Independent Schools 1998 142

Psychology in the Schools 487

Quality Counts* 79

Race Ethnicity and Education 264

Rankings of the States 1995 57

RE:view: Rehabilitation and Education for Blindness and Visual Impairment 303

Reading Abstracts* 49

Reading and Writing Quarterly: Overcoming Learning Difficulties 395

Reading Horizons 396

Reading Improvement 397

Reading Research and Instruction 398

Reading Research Quarterly 399

Reading Teacher 400
Reading World* 398
Religious Education 401
Remedial and Special Education 304
Requirements for Certification of Teach-
    ers, Counselors, Librarians, Ad-
    ministrators for Elementary and
    Secondary Schools, 1998-99 148
Research Centers Directory 1999 190
Research-Doctorate Programs in the
    United States: Continuity and
    Change 209
Research in Education* 50
Research in Higher Education 244
Research in the Teaching of English 402
Research into Higher Education Abstracts
    206
Research Methods in Education and Psy-
    chology: Integrating Diversity
    with Quantitative and Qualitative
    Approaches 443
Research Papers in Education: Policy and
    Practice 99
Resource Guide to Educational Standards
    35
Resources in Education (RIE) 50
Review of Education/Pedagogy/Cultural
    Studies 100
Review of Educational Research 468
Review of Higher Education 245
Review of Research in Education 444
Roeper Review: A Journal on Gifted Edu-
    cation 305
Rural Educator 101

Scandinavian Journal of Educational Re-
    search 469
The Scholarship Advisor 1999 189
School Administrator 421
School Arts 403
School Choice Programs: What's Happen-
    ing in the States 146
School Community Journal 102
School Psychology Review 488
School Review* 70
Science and Children 404
Science Education 405
Science Scope 406
Science Teacher 407
Secondary Teachers Guide to Free Cur-
    riculum Materials 368

Secrets for a Successful Dissertation 197
Slow Learning Child* 292
Social Education 408
Social Studies 409
Sociology of Education 103
Sociology of Education Abstracts 52
Special Education Desk Reference 275
The Special Education Handbook: An In-
    troductory Reference 271
Special Educational Needs Abstracts 283
Speech Teacher* 377
State Education Journal Index, and Educa-
    tors' Guide to Periodicals Re-
    search Strategies 53
State Education Leader 422
Studies in Educational Evaluation 470
Studies in Philosophy and Education 434
Study Abroad 1998-1999 343

T.H.E. Journal 132
Teacher Education and Special Education
    306
Teacher Educator 104
Teachers College Record 105
Teaching and Teacher Education 106
Teaching Education 107
Teaching Exceptional Children 307
Teaching Pre K-8 108
Teaching Tolerance 265
Technological Horizons in Education*
    132
Technology and Learning 133
Technology and Teacher Education An-
    nual, 1996 125
Technology Teacher 134
TechTrends: For Leaders in Education
    and Training 135
TESOL Journal 266
TESOL Quarterly 267
Test Critiques 439
Tests: A Comprehensive Reference for
    Assessments in Psychology, Edu-
    cation and Business 440
Tests in Microfiche 446
Tests in Print IV: An Index to Tests, Test
    Reviews, and the Literature on
    Specific Tests 441
Theory and Research in Social Education
    410
Theory into Practice 109
Thesaurus of ERIC Descriptors 6

Thought and Action 246
Three R's: Race Retention Rates by State
       55
Times Higher Education Supplement 247
Topics in Early Childhood Special Educa-
       tion 308

U. S. Department of Education (ED)
       Home Page 68
U.S. Educational Policy Interest Groups:
       Institutional Profiles 18
UNESCO Statistical Yearbook 1998 347
Universities Quarterly* 227
Urban Education 110

Vocational Aspect of Education* 336

Western European Education* 353
What Every Special Educator Must
       Know: The International Stand-
       ards for the Preparation and Certi-
       fication of Special Education
       Teachers 278
Who's Who in American Education 1996-
       1997 115
World Education Encyclopedia 338
World Education Report 1993 348
World Lecture Hall 317
The World of Learning 191

Yearbook 40
Young Children 162

SUBJECT INDEX

When consulting this index, both the specific term, such as developmental disabilities, and the more general term, such as disabilities, should be considered. Cross-references may be provided, but generally the most specific term is used for terms including "education" and "educational." For example, "educational research" is used rather than "research" and "higher education personnel" is used rather than "personnel." Qualifiers such as "British," "Canadian," and "European" are used for geographic aspects.

abbreviations 12
academic advising 236
academic credentials 192
academic standards 38
   see also: professional standards; standards
accreditation 170
acronyms 12
admissions criteria 192, 196
   see also: college admissions
adult education 309, 310, 314, 318, 319, 321, 323
adult higher education 322
adult literacy 386
adventure-based learning 391
aesthetic education 387
African-American colleges 173
African-American education 253, 261
African American higher education 231
African-Americans 215, 231, 249
agricultural education 331
alcohol education 388
alternative education 314, 315
alternative schools 138
alternative secondary education 141
American Association of Community Colleges 222
American Association of University Professors 214
American education 15
American Educational Research Association 458
American Federation of Teachers 69

American history 374
American Indian colleges 173
American Memory project 374
annual reviews 444
art activities 403
art education 376, 387, 403
assessment 453, 455, 462, 470, 487
   see also: educational measurement; measurement; testing
assessment technology 116
at-risk students 297
Australian education literature 43
author guidelines 37

behavioral disorders 284
behavioral statistics 461
bibliographies 1, 164
bilingual education 254, 255
bilingualism 248
   see also: multilingualism
biographies 111, 112, 113, 114, 115, 163, 435
   see also: early childhood educators; educators
biology education 375
blindness 303
   see also: disabilities; visual impairment
book essays 100
British classroom resources 360
British education 4, 31, 73
British education literature 28, 51
British education organizations 27
British educational research 456

British higher education   227, 247
British special education   285
British special education literature   283
business education   328, 370
business education literature   370

Canadian education   75
Canadian education literature   44
career choice   335
career counseling   325
career development   329, 332
career education   286, 329, 332
career planning materials   326
Carnegie classification   193
Catholic schools   150
certification   148, 325
    see also: licensing; teacher certifica-
        tion; teaching requirements
charter schools   146
child development   153, 156, 486
childhood education   160
Chinese education literature   61
civics   364
classroom activities   88
classroom resources   16, 88, 108, 119,
        121, 123, 145, 326, 357, 359,
        361, 362, 366, 368, 372, 373
    see also: curriculum materials
classroom strategies   96
cognition   475, 480
cognitive sciences   483
college admissions   180, 218, 219
    see also: admissions criteria
college catalogs   194
college courses   194
college degrees   316
college directories   169, 174, 178, 187,
        195, 212
college guides   169, 174, 178, 183, 195
college law   232
    see also: higher education law
college majors   200
college personnel   226
    see also: higher education personnel;
        university personnel
college rankings   198, 199, 213
    see also: rankings: university rankings
college student advising   236
college student research   241
college students   180, 220, 233

college teaching   221
    see also: higher education teaching
colleges and disabilities   274
    see also: disabilities; higher education
        and disabilities
Commonwealth universities   20
communication education   377
communication skills   377
community college research   223, 224
    see also: educational research; higher
        education research
community colleges   171, 210, 222, 223,
        224, 238
    see also: junior colleges
comparative early childhood education   149
comparative education   348, 349, 350,
        351, 354
computer-assisted-instruction   129
computer resources   123
computers   129
contemporary education   79
continuing education   225, 309, 310, 318,
        319, 323
    see also: lifelong education
continuing higher education   322
cooperative education   333
correspondence courses   312
counseling   327, 330, 466
counseling education   481
counseling psychology   481
counseling supervision   481
counselor education   330
current awareness services   45
curricula   356, 379
curriculum analyses   390
curriculum centers   16
curriculum evaluation   356
curriculum history   378
curriculum material reviews   379
curriculum materials   373
    see also: classroom resources
curriculum processes   356
curriculum research   378
curriculum studies   389, 390

developing countries   355
development   29
developmental disabilities   268, 296, 302
    see also: disabilities; mental retardation
developmental education   295
developmental psychology   471, 486

diplomas   196
disabilities   271, 274, 275, 287, 288, 289,
     292, 293, 299, 307
     see also: blindness; colleges and dis-
          abilities; developmental dis-
          abilities; higher education and
          disabilities; learning disabili-
          ties; mental retardation; severe
          disabilities; visual impairment
dissertation process   197, 203
dissertation research   197, 203
distance education   309, 311, 313, 314,
     316, 317, 320, 322, 324
doctoral study   197, 203
doctoral study programs   209
drug education   388

early childhood education   136, 147, 149,
     151, 153, 154, 155, 156, 160, 162
     see also: international early childhood
          education; preschool educa-
          tion; young children
early childhood educators   163
     see also: biographies; educators
early childhood special education   308
     see also: special education
early intervention   296
     see also: special education
economic analyses   414
economics of education   414
education authorship   19
education finance   417
     see also: finance
education indexes   43, 44, 46, 47, 48, 50,
     51, 53, 205, 206, 282, 283, 371,
     413
     see also: educational administration in-
          dexes; physical education in-
          dexes; special education
          indexes
education indicators   346
education information   23
education journal literature   45, 78
education journals   19, 37
education law   201, 412
education literature   1, 28, 33
education of women   87
education organizations   65
     see also: educational associations
education publishing   19
education resources   23, 25, 32

education statistics   57, 58, 59, 66, 69,
     346, 461
     see also: statistics
education systems   338
     see also: national systems of education
education terminology   3, 4, 5, 6, 7, 10,
     31, 270
educational administration   411, 415,
     418, 420, 421
     see also: school administration; school
          system administration; secondary
          school management
educational administration indexes   413
     see also: education indexes
educational associations   23, 41
     see also: education organizations
educational change   34
educational communications   122
educational computer materials   123
educational computing   130
educational credentials   192
educational development   355
educational equity   258
educational essays   100
educational evaluation   447, 454, 470
     see also: evaluation
educational facilities   72
educational foundations   13, 429, 435
educational funding   417
educational history   249, 425, 426, 427,
     430, 431, 432, 433, 435, 472
educational innovations   77
educational issues   76, 80, 81, 89, 91, 93
educational measurement   447, 462
     see also: assessment; measurement;
          testing
educational media   120, 126
educational methodology   442
educational multimedia   117, 118
educational philosophy   423, 428, 429,
     430, 434, 435
educational planning   228
educational policy   18, 29, 73, 79, 81, 83,
     84, 103, 105, 264, 352, 417, 418,
     422, 428
educational practice   30, 109
educational process   13
educational psychology   473, 477, 478,
     479, 482, 483, 488
     see also: learning psychology; school
          psychology

educational reform   29, 33, 34, 35, 38, 146
educational research   24, 25, 30, 32, 40, 97, 99, 410, 436, 442, 443, 444, 449, 450, 454, 456, 457, 458, 459, 460, 461, 463, 464, 465, 467, 468, 469
    see also: community college research; higher education research; learning research; school research; social education research; social studies research; special education research; state education research; teacher education research; vocational research
educational sociology   13, 52, 74
educational software   117, 118
educational studies   40, 84, 89, 429
educational technology   116, 117, 118, 122, 125, 126, 127, 128, 130, 131, 132, 133, 134, 135
educational theory   109, 410, 428, 430
educational video material   119
educators   112, 115
    see also: biographies; early childhood educators
elementary education   140, 151, 157
    see also: primary education
elementary science   404
elementary teaching   96, 108
emotional disorders   284
endowments   172
English for speakers of other languages   256, 266, 267
English for specific purposes   257
English instruction   380, 381
English literature   381
equity   258
ERIC descriptors   6
ERIC gateway   64
ERIC search tools   6, 7
ERIC terminology   6, 7
ERIC thesaurus   6
ethnic studies   250
ethnicity   264
European education   353, 354
evaluation   467, 487
    see also: educational evaluation
evaluation studies   470
evaluation techniques   447
exceptional career development   286

exceptional children   268, 269, 275, 307
    see also: gifted children; giftedness; special education; special needs; talented
exceptional individuals   289
experiential education   391
experimental education   464
experimental educational psychology   478

faculty directories   181
faculty issues   182
federal education information   68
federal legislation   412
feminism   85
finance   172
    see also: education finance
financial aid   188, 189, 202
foreign student enrollment   345
foundations   143
free materials   119, 121, 123, 145, 326, 360, 361, 362, 368
funding   143, 445
funding sources   17, 174

gender studies   85
general education   93
gifted children   290, 291
    see also: exceptional children; giftedness; talented
gifted education   276, 280, 290, 291, 294, 299, 305
giftedness   275, 279, 288, 289, 307
    see also: exceptional children; gifted children; special education; special needs;
government   364
government statistics   58, 59
graduate education programs   176
graduate study   175, 176, 183, 200, 209
grants   17, 143, 172, 186, 445
Great Britain   271
guidance   327
guidance materials   326

high school administration   416
high school education   158
high school study abroad   340
    see also: study abroad

higher education   20, 182, 208, 225, 227, 235, 239, 344, 345
higher education administration   240, 243, 244
higher education administrative officers   185
higher education and disabilities   274
    see also: disabilities; colleges and dis-
        abilities
higher education classification   193
higher education credentials   196
higher education funding   186
higher education history   164, 204
higher education indexes   205, 206
higher education innovations   230
higher education institutions   187, 191
higher education instruction   220, 242
higher education issues   246
higher education journals   216
higher education law   201, 232
    see also: college law
higher education learning   242
higher education literature   205, 206
higher education management   243
higher education newspapers   217, 247
higher education personnel   185
    see also: college personnel; university
        personnel
higher education research   166, 228, 230, 234, 244, 245
    scc also: community college research;
        educational research
higher education statistics   207, 211
higher education teaching   242
    see also: college teaching
historical collections   426
history education   383
history of childhood   427
history of education   425, 427, 431, 433
history teaching   383
human resources management   226

independent schools   138, 141, 142, 159
independent study   312
individual differences   453, 484
    see also: learning differences
industrial education   334
information technology   125, 126
initialisms   12
innovative high school programs   137
innovative practices   77

institutional management   240
institutional research   240
instruction   95, 475
instructional process   480
instructional psychology   471
instructional systems   122
instructional technology   116, 120
integrative studies   177
interdisciplinary studies   177
interest groups   18
interfaith educational research   401
international comparative statistics   346, 348
international development   29
international early childhood education   149
    see also: early childhood education
international education   8, 90, 192, 321, 338, 339, 342, 343, 347, 348, 349, 350, 351, 353
international education literature   48
international education reform   355
international education systems   252
international higher education   165, 167, 168, 179, 344
international history of education   425
international institutions   191
international multicultural education   251, 252
    see also: multicultural education
international scholarships   343
international secondary education pro-
        grams   340
international study   341
    see also: high school study abroad;
        study abroad
international universities   179
Internet classroom resources   359, 372
Internet education information   63
Internet research   128
internships   184

job advertisements   217
junior colleges   171, 210, 238
    see also: community colleges

language arts   380, 393, 396, 402
language instruction indexes   49
language learning   262
language minority students   255

language studies   262
leadership   82
learning   95, 475, 480, 483, 485
learning aids   133
learning differences   484
   see also: individual differences
learning disabilities   272, 298, 301
   see also: disabilities
learning disability measures   277
   see also: measures; tests
learning psychology   482, 484, 485
   see also: educational psychology
learning research   95
   see also: educational research
learning sciences   483
lesson plans   372, 373
liberal education   235
licensing   39
   see also: certification
lifelong education   310
   see also: continuing education
linguistics   259
literacy education   33, 386, 395, 396,
   398, 400
literacy research   365, 399

master's theses   24
mathematics education   129, 358, 382,
   385
mathematics research   385
mathematics resources   366
mathematics standards   366
measurement   439, 440, 441, 442, 451,
   452, 453, 455, 457, 466, 467,
   479
   see also: assessment; educational meas-
      urement; testing
measures   277, 438, 446, 448
   see also: learning disability measures;
      tests
media   119
mental retardation   287, 302
   see also: developmental disabilities;
      disabilities
middle school education   152, 157
middle school science   406
middle schools   161
minorities   215
minority colleges   173
Montessori method   394

motivation   485
multicultural education   110, 251, 258,
   260, 263
   see also: international multicultural
      education; pluralistic education
multicultural higher education   180,
   231
multicultural programs   250
multicultural research   264
multicultural students   180, 254
multiculturalism   265
multilingualism   248, 255, 260
   see also: bilingualism
multimedia   130

National Education Association   41
national higher education systems   165,
   166, 167
national systems of education   339
   see also: education systems
Native Americans, financial aid   188
nonformal education   315, 321

occupational resources   326
open learning   324
opposing viewpoints   109

pedagogy   100
physical education   367, 371
physical education indexes   371
   see also: education indexes
physical fitness   367
pluralistic education   252
   see also: multicultural education
policy analyses   90, 389, 414, 454
policy issues   83, 99, 459
policy research   99
policy studies   97
preschool education   149
   see also: early childhood education
primary education   149
   see also: elementary education
principals   419, 420
private schools   138, 141, 142, 159
professional programs   175
professional standards   148
   see also: academic standards; stand-
      ards; teaching standards
psychological theory   476

psychology journals   37
public policy   18
public school systems   21

qualitative research   443, 460
quantitative methods   443
quotations   11

race   264
race retention rates   55
rankings   56, 198, 199, 209, 213
    see also: college rankings; school rank-
        ings; state education rankings;
        university rankings
reading improvement   397
reading instruction   386, 397, 398, 399,
    400, 402
reading remediation   395
reading research   365, 396, 397, 399,
    400, 402
rehabilitation education   303
rehabilitation terminology   270
religious education   401
remedial education   293, 304
remedial higher education   295
research centers   190
research institutions   193
research literature   468
research methods   436, 443
research programs   190
research support   445
residential facilities for exceptional chil-
    dren   273
resource digests   78
retention rates   55
rural education   101

Scandinavian education   469
scholarships   189, 202
school administration   71, 411, 419, 420,
    421
    see also: educational administration;
        secondary school management
school as community   102
school boards   71
school choice   146
school comparisons   144
school desegregation   424
school directories   60, 67

school districts   139, 140
school locator   67
school psychology   472, 473, 474, 487,
    488
    see also: educational psychology
school rankings   144
    see also: rankings
school readiness   33
school research   102
    see also: educational research
school segregation   424
school supervision   411
school system administration   421
    see also: educational management
school-to-work   286, 333
science education   358, 384, 392, 404,
    405, 406, 407
science education research   363
science instruction   129, 384, 392, 405,
    406, 407
    see also: science teaching
science learning   363, 392
science materials   361
science teaching   363, 384, 392
    see also: science instruction
second language acquisition   257, 262
second language teaching   266
second languages   259
secondary classroom materials   368
secondary education   139, 152, 158
secondary school management   416
    see also: educational administration;
        school administration
secondary science   407
severe disabilities   300
    see also: disabilities
social education research   410
    see also: educational research
social studies   369, 408
social studies education   409
social studies materials   362
social studies research   369, 409
    see also: educational research
social studies teaching   408
sociology of education   52, 103, 352
special education   268, 271, 275, 280,
    289, 292, 293, 395
    see also: early childhood special
        education; early intervention;
        exceptional children; gifted-
        ness; special needs; talented

special education indexes   282, 283
    see also: education indexes
special education information   269
special education research   281
    see also: educational research
special education teaching standards   278
special education terminology   270
special needs   269, 272, 281, 283, 285,
        286, 287, 288, 292, 293, 296,
        298, 299, 300, 301, 302, 303,
        304, 307, 308
    see also: exceptional children; gifted-
        ness; special education;
        talented
special needs facilities   273
special needs programs   273
special needs schools   138, 141, 273
special needs students   297
special needs teaching   306
special teacher education   306
speech instruction   377
staff development in higher education
        229
standards   33, 35, 62, 278, 364, 366
    see also: academic standards; profes-
        sional standards; teaching
        standards
state comparisons   57
state education agencies   22
state education journals   53
state education policy   422
state education rankings   57
    see also: rankings
state education research   53
    see also: educational research
statistical comparisons   56
statistics   58, 59, 67, 150, 207, 208,
        210
    see also: education statistics
student affairs   233, 241
student affairs administration   237
student development   233
study abroad   340, 341, 342, 343, 345
    see also: high school study abroad;
        international study
substance abuse education   388
superintendents   421
supervision   82, 389
systemic reform   35

talented   276, 279, 280, 290, 291, 294,
        305
    see also: exceptional children; gifted
        children; giftedness; special
        education; special needs
teacher certification   39, 148, 278
    see also: certification; teaching
        requirements
teacher concerns   54
teacher development   26
teacher education   2, 42, 92, 94, 104,
        106, 107, 124, 125, 306, 334
teacher education research   42
    see also: educational research
teacher opinions   54
teacher training   42, 92, 94, 104
teachers   26
teaching   2, 26, 106
teaching profession   54
teaching requirements   148
    see also: certification; teacher
        certification
teaching standards   278
    see also: professional standards;
        standards
technical colleges   210
technical education   334
technology   125, 132, 133
technology education   124, 131, 134, 135
test collections   438
test directories   448
testing   219, 451, 452, 453, 455, 462
    see also: assessment; educational meas-
        urement; measurement
tests   277, 438, 439, 440, 441, 446, 448
    see also: learning disability measures;
        measures
textbooks   16, 357, 426
thesis research   203
Title I   297
tolerance   265
training in higher education   229
transition   286
Tribal colleges   173

U.S. Department of Education   68
UNESCO information   90, 347
United Kingdom education organizations
        27

universities   191
university degrees   196
university directories   20, 169, 212
university histories   164, 204
university instruction   221
university personnel   226
    see also: college personnel; higher edu-
        cation personnel
university rankings   198, 199, 213
    see also: college rankings; rankings
university registrars   218
urban education   110

visual impairment   303
    see also: blindness; disabilities
vocational adjustment   335
vocational behavior   335
vocational education   336, 337

vocational research   337
    see also: educational research
vocational training   325, 336, 337
women in higher education   211
women's education   87
work-integrated education   333
world education   338, 348
World Wide Web directories   60, 61, 62,
        63, 64, 65, 66, 67, 68, 212, 213,
        254, 317, 372, 373, 374, 427,
        448
World Wide Web resources   359
writing improvement   395

young children   147, 162
    see also: early childhood education